War and Peace

*A collection of classic
poetry and prose*

INTRODUCED BY

Michael Morpurgo

EDITED BY

Kate Agnew

Published in the UK in 2004 by Wizard Books Ltd.,
an imprint of Icon Books Ltd.,
The Old Dairy, Brook Road, Thriplow,
Cambridge SG8 7RG
e-mail: wizard@iconbooks.co.uk
www.iconbooks.co.uk/wizard

Sold in the UK, Europe, South Africa
and Asia by Faber and Faber Ltd.,
3 Queen Square, London WC1N 3AU
or their agents

Distributed in the UK, Europe, South Africa
and Asia by TBS Ltd., Frating Distribution Centre,
Colchester Road, Frating Green, Colchester CO7 7DW

Published in Australia in 2004
by Allen & Unwin Pty. Ltd.,
PO Box 8500, 83 Alexander Street,
Crows Nest, NSW 2065

Distributed in Canada by
Penguin Books Canada,
10 Alcorn Avenue, Suite 300,
Toronto, Ontario M4V 3B2

ISBN 1 84046 570 0

Typesetting by Wayzgoose

Printed and bound in the UK by Bookmarque

Kate Agnew read English at the University of Oxford, has chaired the Children's Booksellers Association and has served as a judge for the Smarties Prize and the Whitbread Award. She was a contributor to the *Cambridge Guide to Children's Books* and co-wrote *Children at War* with Geoff Fox. In 1999 she won a special British Book Award for her contribution to the National Year of Reading.

Michael Morpurgo is the Children's Laureate and has published over 95 titles. His books have been translated into over twenty languages; many have been adapted for the theatre and five have been made into films. In 1999 he was awarded an MBE for services to youth. His books have won the Whitbread Award, the Smarties Book Prize, the Children's Book Award and the Cercle D'Or Prix Sorcière (France). Several have been shortlisted for the Carnegie Medal.

Contents

Introduction

I was born in 1943, in the middle of the Second World War. I grew up with the destruction of this war all around me. I saw it in the bombsites I played in, I heard it in the sad voices of my parents and their friends whenever they spoke of it. I heard their stories, looked at family photographs of men in uniform, my uncle Peter in particular who had been in the RAF and had been shot down and killed in 1941. His eyes looked back at the nephew he had never met. For me he never grew old, like I did, like everyone else did. He's still young in my mind even to this day.

When I became a writer I found myself naturally drawn to the subject of war because of how it had affected my growing up, I'm sure, because I had seen the damage of it close up, wondered at the courage of those who fought, witnessed the enduring grief of the survivors, the pain that never goes away. I write stories about war never to entertain but perhaps to explore my own feelings about it.

Many of those whose work you'll read here were doing the same thing their way. Many had lived through it and fought in it. Some died in it. Here are poets and writers who came face to face with the terror and the triumph and the pity too; or like me, never witnessed it themselves but needed to come to terms with how men and women had endured the heat of battle and shared the grief.

I myself have been lucky, like most of my generation. I have lived through sixty years and never been to war, never had war come to me. We could be deceived into believing the horror of it is a thing of the past, not relevant to us today. Sadly, we know this not to be true. It is simply happening further away, endured by others, but brought daily to us on our television screens and sanitized for us so we don't have to feel too uncomfortable. It is through the literature you'll find in this book we can all come to a closer understanding of war – how it is to fight it, to live through it, the pain and the pity of it. Only with this kind of understanding universally shared can we one day perhaps really make war a thing of the past.

Michael Morpugo, *June 2004*

Friends and
Enemies

A Poison Tree

I was angry with my friend;
I told my wrath, my wrath did end.
I was angry with my foe;
I told it not, my wrath did grow.

And I watered it in fears,
Night and morning with my tears;
And I sunned it with smiles,
And with soft deceitful wiles.

And it grew both day and night
Till it bore an apple bright –
And my foe beheld it shine.
And he knew that it was mine,

And into my garden stole,
When the night had veiled the pole.
In the morning glad I see
My foe outstretched beneath the tree.

Songs of Experience
William Blake (1757–1827)

The Arrow and the Song

I shot an arrow into the air,
It fell to earth, I knew not where;
For, so swiftly it flew, the sight
Could not follow it in its flight.

I breathed a song into the air,
It fell to earth, I knew not where;
For who has sight so keen and strong
That it can follow the flight of song?

Long, long afterward, in an oak
I found the arrow, still unbroke;
And the song, from beginning to end,
I found again in the heart of a friend.

Henry Wadsworth Longfellow (1807–82)

The Peace-Offering

It was but a little thing,
Yet I knew it meant to me
Ease from what had given a sting
To the very birdsinging
    Latterly.

But I would not welcome it;
And for all I then declined
O the regrettings infinite
When the night-processions flit
    Through the mind!

Thomas Hardy (1840–1928)

Strange Meeting

It seemed that out of battle I escaped
Down some profound dull tunnel, long since scooped
Through granites which titanic wars had groined.

Yet also there encumbered sleepers groaned,
Too fast in thought or death to be bestirred.
Then, as I probed them, one sprang up, and stared
With piteous recognition in fixed eyes,
Lifting distressful hands, as if to bless.
And by his smile, I knew that sullen hall, –
By his dead smile I knew we stood in hell.

With a thousand pains that vision's face was grained;
Yet no blood reached there from the upper ground,
And no guns thumped, or down the flues made moan.
'Strange friend,' I said, 'here is no cause to mourn.'
'None,' said that other, 'save the undone years,
The hopelessness. Whatever hope is yours,
Was my life also; I went hunting wild
After the wildest beauty in the world,
Which lies not calm in eyes, or braided hair,
But mocks the steady running of the hour,
And if it grieves, grieves richlier than here.
For by my glee might many men have laughed,
And of my weeping something had been left,
Which must die now. I mean the truth untold,
The pity of war, the pity war distilled.
Now men will go content with what we spoiled,
Or, discontent, boil bloody, and be spilled.

They will be swift with swiftness of the tigress.
None will break ranks, though nations trek from progress.
Courage was mine, and I had mystery,
Wisdom was mine, and I had mastery:
To miss the march of this retreating world
Into vain citadels that are not walled.
Then, when much blood had clogged their chariot-wheels,
I would go up and wash them from sweet wells,
Even with truths that lie too deep for taint.
I would have poured my spirit without stint
But not through wounds; not on the cess of war.
Foreheads of men have bled where no wounds were.
I am the enemy you killed, my friend.
I knew you in this dark: for so you frowned
Yesterday through me as you jabbed and killed.
I parried; but my hands were loath and cold.
Let us sleep now ...'

Wilfred Owen (1893–1918)

This is No Case of Petty Right or Wrong

This is no case of petty right or wrong
That politicians or philosophers
Can judge. I hate not Germans, nor grow hot
With love of Englishmen, to please newspapers.
Beside my hate for one fat patriot
My hatred of the Kaiser is love true: –
A kind of god he is, banging a gong.
But I have not to choose between the two,
Or between justice and injustice. Dinned
With war and argument I read no more
Than in the storm smoking along the wind
Athwart the wood. Two witches' cauldrons roar.
From one the weather shall rise clear and gay;
Out of the other an England beautiful
And like her mother that died yesterday.
Little I know or care if, being dull,
I shall miss something that historians
Can rake out of the ashes when perchance
The phoenix broods serene above their ken.
But with the best and meanest Englishmen
I am one in crying, God save England, lest
We lose what never slaves and cattle blessed.
The ages made her that made us from dust:
She is all we know and live by, and we trust
She is good and must endure, loving her so:
And as we love ourselves we hate her foe.

Edward Thomas (1878–1917)

Shiloh

A Requiem

Skimming lightly, wheeling still,
  The swallows fly low
Over the field in clouded days,
  The forest-field of Shiloh –
Over the field where April rain
Solaced the parched ones stretched in pain
Through the pause of night
That followed the Sunday fight
  Around the church of Shiloh –
The church so lone, the log-built one,
That echoed to many a parting groan
  And natural prayer
Of dying foemen mingled there –
Foemen at morn, but friends at eve –
Fame or country least their care:
(What like a bullet can undeceive!)
  But now they lie low,
While over them the swallows skim,
  And all is hushed at Shiloh.

Herman Melville (1819–1891)

Aeneas Tells of the Wooden Horse

All were attentive to the godlike man,
When from his lofty couch he thus began:
'Great queen, what you command me to relate
Renews the sad remembrance of our fate:
An empire from its old foundations rent,
And every woe the Trojans underwent;
A peopled city made a desert place;
All that I saw, and part of which I was:
Not even the hardest of our foes could hear,
Nor stern Ulysses tell without a tear.
And now the latter watch of wasting night,
And setting stars, to kindly rest invite;
But, since you take such interest in our woe,
And Troy's disastrous end desire to know,
I will restrain my tears, and briefly tell
What in our last and fatal night befell.
By destiny compelled, and in despair,
The Greeks grew weary of the tedious war,
And by Minerva's aid a fabric reared,
Which like a steed of monstrous height appeared:
The sides were planked with pine; they feigned it made
For their return, and this the vow they paid.
Thus they pretend, but in the hollow side
Selected numbers of their soldiers hide:
With inward arms the dire machine they load,
And iron bowels stuff the dark abode.
In sight of Troy lies Tenedos, an isle
(While Fortune did on Priam's empire smile)
Renowned for wealth; but, since, a faithless bay,

Where ships exposed to wind and weather lay.
There was their fleet concealed. We thought, for Greece
Their sails were hoisted, and our fears release.
The Trojans, cooped within their walls so long,
Unbar their gates, and issue in a throng,
Like swarming bees, and with delight survey
The camp deserted, where the Grecians lay:
The quarters of the several chiefs they showed;
Here Phoenix, here Achilles, made abode;
Here joined the battles; there the navy rode.
Part on the pile their wondering eyes employ:
The pile by Pallas raised to ruin Troy.
Thymoetes first ('tis doubtful whether hired,
Or so the Trojan destiny required)
Moved that the ramparts might be broken down,
To lodge the monster fabric in the town.
But Capys, and the rest of sounder mind,
The fatal present to the flames designed,
Or to the watery deep; at least to bore
The hollow sides, and hidden frauds explore.
The giddy vulgar, as their fancies guide,
With noise say nothing, and in parts divide.
Laocoon, followed by a numerous crowd,
Ran from the fort, and cried, from far, aloud:
'O wretched countrymen! What fury reigns?
What more than madness has possessed your brains?
Think you the Grecians from your coasts are gone?
And are Ulysses' arts no better known?
This hollow fabric either must enclose,
Within its blind recess, our secret foes;
Or 'tis an engine raised above the town,

To o'erlook the walls, and then to batter down.
Somewhat is sure designed, by fraud or force:
Trust not their presents, nor admit the horse.'
Thus having said, against the steed he threw
His forceful spear, which, hissing as it flew,
Pierced through the yielding planks of jointed wood,
And trembling in the hollow belly stood.
The sides, transpierced, return a rattling sound,
And groans of Greeks enclosed come issuing through the
   wound
And, had not Heaven the fall of Troy designed,
Or had not men been fated to be blind,
Enough was said and done t'inspire a better mind.
Then had our lances pierced the treacherous wood,
And Ilian towers and Priam's empire stood.'

The Aeneid, Book II
Virgil (70–19 BC)
Translated by John Dryden (1631–1700)

Once There Came a Man

Once there came a man
Who said,
'Range me all men of the world in rows.'
And instantly
There was terrific clamour among the people
Against being ranged in rows.
There was a loud quarrel, world-wide.
It endured for ages;
And blood was shed
By those who pined to stand in rows.
Eventually, the man went to death, weeping.
And those who stayed in bloody scuffle
Knew not the great simplicity.

Stephen Crane (1871–1900)

The Soldier

Yes. Why do we all, seeing of a soldier, bless him? Bless
Our redcoats, our tars? Both these being, the greater part,
But frail clay, nay but foul clay. Here it is: the heart,
Since, proud, it calls the calling manly, gives a guess
That, hopes that, makes believe, the men must be no less;
It fancies, feigns, deems, dears the artist after his art;
And fain will find as sterling all as all is smart,
And scarlet wear the spirit of wár thére express.

Mark Christ our King. He knows war, served this soldiering
   through;
He of all can handle a rope best. There he bides in bliss
Now, and séeing somewhére some mán do all that man can do,
For love he leans forth, needs his neck must fall on, kiss,
And cry 'O Christ-done deed! So God-made-flesh does too:
Were I come o'er again' cries Christ 'it should be this.'

Gerard Manley Hopkins (1844–89)

The Regiment Prepares to Leave Meryton

The first week of their return was soon gone. The second began. It was the last of the regiment's stay in Meryton, and all the young ladies in the neighbourhood were drooping apace. The dejection was almost universal. The elder Miss Bennets alone were still able to eat, drink, and sleep, and pursue the usual course of their employments. Very frequently were they reproached for this insensibility by Kitty and Lydia, whose own misery was extreme, and who could not comprehend such hard-heartedness in any of the family.

'Good Heaven! What is to become of us! What are we to do!' would they often exclaim in the bitterness of woe. 'How can you be smiling so, Lizzy?'

Their affectionate mother shared all their grief; she remembered what she had herself endured on a similar occasion, five and twenty years ago.

'I am sure,' said she, 'I cried for two days together when Colonel Millar's regiment went away. I thought I should have broke my heart.'

'I am sure I shall break *mine*,' said Lydia.

'If one could but go to Brighton!' observed Mrs. Bennet.

'Oh, yes! – if one could but go to Brighton! But papa is so disagreeable.'

'A little sea-bathing would set me up for ever.'

'And my aunt Philips is sure it would do me a great deal of good,' added Kitty.

Such were the kind of lamentations resounding perpetually through Longbourn House. Elizabeth tried to be diverted by them; but all sense of pleasure was lost in shame. She felt anew the justice of Mr. Darcy's objections; and never had she before been so much disposed to pardon his interference in the views of his friend.

But the gloom of Lydia's prospect was shortly cleared away; for she received an invitation from Mrs. Forster, the wife of the Colonel of the regiment, to accompany her to Brighton. This invaluable friend was a very young woman, and very lately married. A resemblance in good humour and good spirits had recommended her and Lydia to each other, and out of their *three* months' acquaintance they had been intimate *two*.

Pride and Prejudice
Jane Austen (1775–1817)

The Eve of Waterloo

There was a sound of revelry by night,
  And Belgium's capital had gathered then
  Her beauty and her chivalry, and bright
  The lamps shone o'er fair women and brave men.
  A thousand hearts beat happily; and when
  Music arose with its voluptuous swell,
  Soft eyes looked love to eyes which spake again,
  And all went merry as a marriage bell;
But hush! hark! a deep sound strikes like a rising knell!

Did ye not hear it? – No; 'twas but the wind,
  Or the car rattling o'er the stony street;
  On with the dance! let joy be unconfined;
  No sleep till morn, when youth and pleasure meet
  To chase the glowing hours with flying feet.
  But hark! – that heavy sound breaks in once more,
  As if the clouds its echo would repeat;
  And nearer, clearer, deadlier than before;
Arm! arm! it is – it is – the cannon's opening roar!

Within a windowed niche of that high hall
  Sat Brunswick's fated chieftain; he did hear
  That sound the first amidst the festival,
  And caught its tone with Death's prophetic ear;
  And when they smiled because he deemed it near,
  His heart more truly knew that peal too well
  Which stretched his father on a bloody bier,
  And roused the vengeance blood alone could quell;
He rushed into the field, and, foremost fighting, fell.

Ah! then and there was hurrying to and fro,
  And gathering tears, and tremblings of distress,
  And cheeks all pale, which, but an hour ago,
  Blushed at the praise of their own loveliness.
  And there were sudden partings, such as press
  The life from out young hearts, and choking sighs
  Which ne'er might be repeated; who would guess
  If ever more should meet those mutual eyes,
Since upon night so sweet such awful morn could rise!

And there was mounting in hot haste; the steed,
  The mustering squadron, and the clattering car,
  Went pouring forward with impetuous speed,
  And swiftly forming in the ranks of war;
  And the deep thunder, peal on peal afar;
  And near, the beat of the alarming drum
  Roused up the soldier ere the morning star;
  While thronged the citizens with terror dumb,
Or whispering, with white lips – 'The foe! They come! They come!'

Childe Harold's Pilgrimage
George Gordon, Lord Byron (1788–1824)

The Duchess of Richmond's Ball

There never was, since the days of Darius, such a brilliant train of camp-followers as hung round the Duke of Wellington's army in the Low Countries, in 1815; and led it dancing and feasting, as it were, up to the very brink of battle. A certain ball which a noble Duchess gave at Brussels on the 15th of June in the above-named year is historical. All Brussels had been in a state of excitement about it, and I have heard from ladies who were in that town at the period, that the talk and interest of persons of their own sex regarding the ball was much greater even than in respect of the enemy in their front. The struggles, intrigues, and prayers to get tickets were such as only English ladies will employ, in order to gain admission to the society of the great of their own nation ...

On the appointed night, George, having commanded new dresses and ornaments of all sorts for Amelia, drove to the famous ball, where his wife did not know a single soul. After looking about for Lady Bareacres, who cut him, thinking the card was quite enough – and after placing Amelia on a bench, he left her to her own cogitations there, thinking, on his own part, that he had behaved very handsomely in getting her new clothes, and bringing her to the ball, where she was free to amuse herself as she liked. Her thoughts were not of the pleasantest, and nobody except honest Dobbin came to disturb them.

Whilst her appearance was an utter failure (as her husband felt with a sort of rage), Mrs Rawdon Crawley's *début* was, on the contrary, very brilliant. She arrived very late. Her face was radiant; her dress perfection. In the midst of the great persons assembled, and the eye-glasses directed to her, Rebecca seemed to be as cool and collected as when she used to marshal Miss Pinkerton's little girls to church. Numbers of the men she knew already, and the dandies thronged round her. As for the ladies, it was whispered among them that Rawdon had run away with her from out of a convent, and that she was a relation of the Montmorency family. She spoke French so perfectly that there might be some truth in this report, and it was agreed that her manners were fine, and her air *distingue*. Fifty would-be partners thronged round her at once, and pressed to have the honour to dance with her. But she said she was engaged, and only going to dance very little; and made her way at once to the place where Emmy sat quite unnoticed, and dismally unhappy. And so, to finish the poor child at once, Mrs Rawdon ran and greeted affectionately her dearest Amelia, and began forthwith to patronise her. She found fault with her friend's dress, and her hairdresser, and wondered how she could be so *chaussee*, and vowed that she must send her *corsetiere* the next morning. She vowed that it was a delightful ball; that there was everybody that every one knew, and only a *very* few nobodies in the whole room. It is a fact, that in a fortnight, and after three dinners in general society, this young woman had got up the genteel jargon so well, that a native could not speak it better; and it was only from her French being so good, that you could know she was not a born woman of fashion.

George, who had left Emmy on her bench on entering the ball-room, very soon found his way back when Rebecca was by her dear friend's side. Becky was just lecturing Mrs Osborne upon the follies which her husband was committing. 'For God's sake, stop him from gambling, my dear,' she said, 'or he will ruin himself. He and Rawdon are playing at cards every night, and you know he is very poor, and

Rawdon will win every shilling from him if he does not take care. Why don't you prevent him, you little careless creature? Why don't you come to us of an evening, instead of moping at home with that Captain Dobbin? I dare say he is *tres aimable*; but how could one love a man with feet of such size? Your husband's feet are darlings – Here he comes. Where have you been, wretch? Here is Emmy crying her eyes out for you. Are you coming to fetch me for the quadrille?' And she left her bouquet and shawl by Amelia's side, and tripped off with George to dance. Women only know how to wound so. There is a poison on the tips of their little shafts, which stings a thousand times more than a man's blunter weapon. Our poor Emmy, who had never hated, never sneered all her life, was powerless in the hands of her remorseless little enemy …

At last George came back for Rebecca's shawl and flowers. She was going away. She did not even condescend to come back and say good-bye to Amelia. The poor girl let her husband come and go without saying a word, and her head fell on her breast. Dobbin had been called away, and was whispering deep in conversation with the General of the division, his friend, and had not seen this last parting. George went away then with the bouquet; but when he gave it to the owner, there lay a note, coiled like a snake among the flowers. Rebecca's eye caught it at once. She had been used to deal with notes in early life. She put out her hand and took the nosegay. He saw by her eyes as they met, that she was aware what she should find there. Her husband hurried her away, still too intent upon his own thoughts, seemingly, to take note of any marks of recognition which might pass between his friend and his wife. These were, however, but trifling. Rebecca gave George her hand with one of her usual quick knowing glances, and made a curtsey and walked away. George bowed over the hand, said nothing in reply to a remark of Crawley's, did not hear it even, his brain was so throbbing with triumph and excitement, and allowed them to go away without a word.

His wife saw the one part at least of the bouquet-scene. It was quite natural that George should come at Rebecca's request to get her her scarf and flowers: it was no more than he had done twenty times before in the course of the last few days; but now it was too much for her. 'William,' she said, suddenly clinging to Dobbin, who was near her, 'you've always been very kind to me – I'm – I'm not well. Take me home.' She did not know she called him by his Christian name, as George was accustomed to do. He went away with her quickly. Her lodgings were hard by; and they threaded through the crowd without, where everything seemed to be more astir than even in the ballroom within.

George had been angry twice or thrice at finding his wife up on his return from the parties which he frequented: so she went straight to bed now; but although she did not sleep, and although the din and clatter, and the galloping of horsemen were incessant, she never heard any of these noises, having quite other disturbances to keep her awake.

Osborne meanwhile, wild with elation, went off to a play-table, and began to bet frantically. He won repeatedly. 'Everything succeeds with me tonight,' he said. But his luck at play even did not cure him of his restlessness, and he started up after awhile, pocketing his winnings, and went to a buffet, where he drank off many bumpers of wine.

Here, as he was rattling away to the people around, laughing loudly and wild with spirits, Dobbin found him. He had been to the card-tables to look there for his friend.

Dobbin looked as pale and grave as his comrade was flushed and jovial.

'Hullo, Dob! Come and drink, old Dob! The Duke's wine is famous. Give me some more, you sir'; and he held out a trembling glass for the liquor.

'Come out, George,' said Dobbin, still gravely; 'don't drink.'

'Drink! there's nothing like it. Drink yourself, and light up your lantern jaws, old boy. Here's to you.'

Dobbin went up and whispered something to him, at which George, giving a start and a wild hurray, tossed off his glass, clapped it on the table, and walked away speedily on his friend's arm. 'The enemy has passed the Sambre,' William said, 'and our left is already engaged. Come away. We are to march in three hours.'

Away went George, his nerves quivering with excitement at the news so long looked for, so sudden when it came. What were love and intrigue now? He thought about a thousand things but these in his rapid walk to his quarters – his past life and future chances – the fate which might be before him – the wife, the child perhaps, from whom unseen he might be about to part. Oh, how he wished that night's work undone! and that with a clear conscience at least he might say farewell to the tender and guileless being by whose love he had set such little store!

Vanity Fair
William Makepeace Thackeray (1811–63)

Othello's Courtship

Her father loved me, oft invited me;
Still questioned me the story of my life
From year to year – the battles, sieges, fortunes,
That I have passed.
I ran it through, even from my boyish days
To the very moment that he bade me tell it;
Wherein I spake of most disastrous chances,
Of moving accidents by flood and field;
Of hairbreadth scapes in the imminent deadly breach;
Of being taken by the insolent foe
And sold to slavery; of my redemption thence,
And portance in my travel's history;
Wherein of antres vast and deserts idle,
Rough quarries, rocks and hills whose heads touch heaven,
It was my hint to speak – such was the process;
And of the Cannibals that each other eat,
The Anthropophagi and men whose heads
Do grow beneath their shoulders. This to hear
Would Desdemona seriously incline;
But still the house affairs would draw her thence;
Which ever as she could with haste dispatch,
She'd come again, and with a greedy ear
Devour up my discourse. Which I observing,
Took once a pliant hour, and found good means
To draw from her a prayer of earnest heart
That I would all my pilgrimage dilate,
Whereof by parcels she had something heard,
But not intentively. I did consent,
And often did beguile her of her tears,

When I did speak of some distressful stroke
That my youth suffered. My story being done,
She gave me for my pains a world of sighs;
She swore, in faith, 'twas strange, 'twas passing strange;
'Twas pitiful, 'twas wondrous pitiful.
She wished she had not heard it; yet she wished
That heaven had made her such a man. She thanked me;
And bade me, if I had a friend that loved her,
I should but teach him how to tell my story,
And that would woo her. Upon this hint I spake;
She loved me for the dangers I had passed;
And I loved her that she did pity them.
This only is the witchcraft I have used.
Here comes the lady; let her witness it.

Othello, Act 1 Scene 3
William Shakespeare (1564–1616)

A Farewell to Arms
To Queen Elizabeth

His golden locks Time hath to silver turned;
   O Time too swift, O swiftness never ceasing!
His youth 'gainst time and age hath ever spurned,
   But spurned in vain; youth waneth by increasing:
Beauty, strength, youth, are flowers but fading seen;
Duty, faith, love, are roots, and ever green.

His helmet now shall make a hive for bees;
   And, lovers' sonnets turned to holy psalms,
A man-at-arms must now serve on his knees,
   And feed on prayers, which are Age his alms:
But though from court to cottage he depart,
His Saint is sure of his unspotted heart.

And when he saddest sits in homely cell,
   He'll teach his swains this carol for a song, –
'Blest be the hearts that wish my sovereign well,
   Curst be the souls that think her any wrong.'
Goddess, allow this agèd man his right
To be your beadsman now that was your knight.

George Peele (1556–96)

Leaders and
Leadership

Once More Unto the Breach

Once more unto the breach, dear friends, once more;
Or close the wall up with our English dead.
In peace there's nothing so becomes a man
As modest stillness and humility;
But when the blast of war blows in our ears,
Then imitate the action of the tiger:
Stiffen the sinews, summon up the blood,
Disguise fair nature with hard-favoured rage;
Then lend the eye a terrible aspect;
Let it pry through the portage of the head
Like the brass cannon; let the brow overwhelm it
As fearfully as doth a galled rock
Overhang and jutty his confounded base,
Swilled with the wild and wasteful ocean.
Now set the teeth and stretch the nostril wide;
Hold hard the breath, and bend up every spirit
To his full height. On, on, you noblest English,
Whose blood is fet from fathers of war-proof –
Fathers that like so many Alexanders
Have in these parts from morn till even fought,
And sheathed their swords for lack of argument.
Dishonour not your mothers; now attest
That those whom you called fathers did beget you.
Be copy now to men of grosser blood,
And teach them how to war. And you, good yeomen,
Whose limbs were made in England, show us here
The mettle of your pasture; let us swear
That you are worth your breeding – which I doubt not;
For there is none of you so mean and base

That hath not noble lustre in your eyes.
I see you stand like greyhounds in the slips,
Straining upon the start. The game's afoot:
Follow your spirit; and upon this charge
Cry 'God for Harry, England, and Saint George!'

King Henry V, Act 3 Scene 1
William Shakespeare (1564–1616)

Agincourt

Fair stood the wind for France
When we our sails advance,
Nor now to prove our chance
   Longer will tarry;
But putting to the main,
At Caux, the mouth of Seine,
With all his martial train
   Landed King Harry.

And taking many a fort,
Furnished in warlike sort,
Marcheth towards Agincourt
   In happy hour;
Skirmishing day by day
With those that stopped his way,
Where the French general lay
   With all his power.

Which, in his height of pride,
King Henry to deride,
His ransom to provide
   Unto him sending;
Which he neglects the while
As from a nation vile,
Yet with an angry smile
   Their fall portending.

And turning to his men,
Quoth our brave Henry then,

'Though they to one be ten
   Be not amazèd:
Yet have we well begun;
Battles so bravely won
Have ever to the sun
   By fame been raisèd.

'And for myself (quoth he):
This my full rest shall be:
England never mourn for me
   Nor more esteem me:
Victor I will remain
Or on this earth lie slain,
Never shall she sustain
   Loss to redeem me.

'Poitiers and Cressy tell,
When most their pride did swell,
Under our swords they fell:
   No less our skill is
Than when our grandsire great,
Claiming the regal seat,
By many a warlike feat
   Lopped the French lilies.'

The Duke of York so dread
The eager vaward led;
With the main Henry sped
   Among his henchmen.
Excester had the rear,

A braver man not there;
O Lord, how hot they were
  On the false Frenchmen!

They now to fight are gone,
Armour on armour shone,
Drum now to drum did groan,
  To hear was wonder;
That with the cries they make
The very earth did shake:
Trumpet to trumpet spake,
  Thunder to thunder.

Well it thine age became,
O noble Erpingham,
Which didst the signal aim
  To our hid forces!
When from a meadow by,
Like a storm suddenly
The English archery
  Stuck the French horses.

With Spanish yew so strong,
Arrows a cloth-yard long
That like to serpents stung,
  Piercing the weather;
None from his fellow starts,
But playing manly parts,
And like true English hearts
  Stuck close together.

When down their bows they threw,
And forth their bilbos drew,
And on the French they flew,
    Not one was tardy;
Arms were from shoulders sent,
Scalps to the teeth were rent,
Down the French peasants went –
    Our men were hardy!

This while our noble king,
His broadsword brandishing,
Down the French host did ding
    As to o'erwhelm it;
And many a deep wound lent,
His arms with blood besprent,
And many a cruel dent
    Bruised his helmet.

Gloucester, that duke so good,
Next of the royal blood,
For famous England stood
    With his brave brother;
Clarence, in steel so bright,
Though but a maiden knight,
Yet in that furious fight
    Scarce such another.

Warwick in blood did wade,
Oxford the foe invade,
And cruel slaughter made
    Still as they ran up;

Suffolk his axe did ply,
Beaumont and Willoughby
Bare them right doughtily,
    Ferrers and Fanhope.

Upon Saint Crispin's Day
Fought was this noble fray,
Which fame did not delay
    To England to carry.
O when shall English men
With such acts fill a pen?
Or England breed again
    Such a King Harry?

Michael Drayton (1563–1631)

Satan Rallies His Troops

What though the field be lost?
All is not lost; the unconquerable will,
And study of revenge, immortal hate,
And courage never to submit or yield:
And what is else not to be overcome?
That glory never shall his wrath or might
Extort from me. To bow and sue for grace
With suppliant knee, and deify his power,
Who from the terror of this arm so late
Doubted his empire, that were low indeed,
That were an ignominy and shame beneath
This downfall; since by fate the strength of gods
And this empyreal substance cannot fail,
Since through experience of this great event
In arms not worse, in foresight much advanced,
We may with more successful hope resolve
To wage by force or guile eternal war
Irreconcilable, to our grand foe,
Who now triumphs, and in the excess of joy
Sole reigning holds the tyranny of heaven.

Paradise Lost, Book I
John Milton (1608–74)

On the Lord General Fairfax
at the Siege of Colchester

Fairfax, whose name in arms through Europe rings
  Filling each mouth with envy, or with praise,
  And all her jealous monarchs with amaze,
  And rumours loud, that daunt remotest kings,
Thy firm unshaken virtue ever brings
  Victory home, though new rebellions raise
  Their hydra heads, and the false North displays
  Her broken league, to imp their serpent wings,
O yet a nobler task awaits thy hand;
  For what can war, but endless war still breed,
  Till truth, and right from violence be freed,
And public faith cleared from the shameful brand
  Of public fraud. In vain doth valour bleed
  While avarice, and rapine share the land.

John Milton (1608–74)

An Horatian Ode Upon Cromwell's Return from Ireland

The forward youth that would appear
Must now forsake his muses dear,
    Nor in the shadows sing
    His numbers languishing.
'Tis time to leave the books in dust,
And oil the unused armour's rust,
    Removing from the wall
    The corslet of the hall.
So restless Cromwell could not cease
In the inglorious arts of peace,
    But through adventurous war
    Urgèd his active star:
And like the three-forked lightning, first
Breaking the clouds where it was nursed,
    Did thorough his own side
    His fiery way divide:
For 'tis all one to courage high,
The emulous or enemy;
    And with such to enclose
    Is more than to oppose.
Then burning through the air he went
And palaces and temples rent;
    And Caesar's head at last
    Did through his laurels blast.
'Tis madness to resist or blame
The face of angry Heaven's flame;
    And, if we would speak true,
    Much to the man is due.

Who, from his private gardens, where
He lived reservèd and austere
  As if his highest plot
  To plant the bergamot,
Could by industrious valour climb
To ruin the great work of time,
  And cast the kingdoms old
  Into another mould;
Though Justice against Fate complain,
And plead the ancient rights in vain –
  But those do hold or break
  As men are strong or weak.
Nature, that hateth emptiness,
Allows of penetration less,
  And therefore must make room
  Where greater spirits come.
What field of all the civil war
Where his were not the deepest scar?
  And Hampton shows what part
  He had of wiser art;
Where, twining subtle fears with hope,
He wove a net of such a scope
  That Charles himself might chase
  To Carisbrook's narrow case;
That thence the royal actor borne
The tragic scaffold might adorn:
  While round the armèd bands
  Did clap their bloody hands.
He nothing common did or mean
Upon that memorable scene,
  But with his keener eye
  The axe's edge did try;

Nor called the gods, with vulgar spite,
To vindicate his helpless right;
  But bowed his comely head
  Down, as upon a bed.
This was that memorable hour
Which first assured the forcèd power:
  So when they did design
  The capitol's first line,
A bleeding head, where they begun,
Did fright the architects to run;
  And yet in that the State
  Foresaw its happy fate!
And now the Irish are ashamed
To see themselves in one year tamed:
  So much one man can do
  That does both act and know.
They can affirm his praises best,
And have, though overcome, confessed
  How good he is, how just
  And fit for highest trust;
Nor yet grown stiffer with command,
But still in the Republic's hand –
  How fit he is to sway
  That can so well obey!
He to the Commons' feet presents
A kingdom for his first year's rents,
  And, what he may, forbears
  His fame, to make it theirs:
And has his sword and spoils ungirt
To lay them at the public's skirt.
  So when the falcon high
  Falls heavy from the sky,

She, having killed, no more does search
But on the next green bough to perch,
    Where, when he first does lure,
    The falconer has her sure.
What may not then our isle presume
While victory his crest does plume?
    What may not others fear,
    If thus he crowns each year?
As Caesar he, ere long, to Gaul,
To Italy an Hannibal,
    And to all States not free
    Shall climacteric be.
The Pict no shelter now shall find
Within his particoloured mind,
    But, from this valour, sad
    Shrink underneath the plaid,
Happy, if in the tufted brake
The English hunter him mistake,
    Nor lay his hounds in near
    The Caledonian deer.
But thou, the Wars' and Fortune's son,
March indefatigably on;
    And for the last effect,
    Still keep the sword erect:
Besides the force it has to fright
The spirits of the shady night,
    The same arts that did gain
    A power, must it maintain.

                        Andrew Marvell (1621–78)

Rudiments of War

TAMBURLAINE

Villain, art thou the son of Tamburlaine,
And fearest to die, or with a curtle-axe
To hew thy flesh, and make a gaping wound?
Hast thou beheld a peal of ordnance strike
A ring of pikes, mingled with shot and horse,
Whose shattered limbs, being tossed as high as heaven,
Hang in the air as thick as sunny motes,
And canst thou, coward, stand in fear of death?
Hast thou not seen my horsemen charge the foe,
Shot through the arms, cut overthwart the hands,
Dying their lances with their streaming blood,
And yet at night carouse within my tent,
Filling their empty veins with airy wine,
That, being concocted, turns to crimson blood,
And wilt thou shun the field for fear of wounds?
View me, thy father, that hath conquered kings,
And, with his host, marched round about the earth,
Quite void of scars and clear from any wound,
That by the wars lost not a drop of blood,
And see him lance his flesh to teach you all.
[*He cuts his arm*]
A wound is nothing, be it never so deep;
Blood is the God of War's rich livery ...

Tamburlaine, Act 3 Scene 2
Christopher Marlowe (1564–93)

The Deeds of Coriolanus

COMINIUS

    ... the deeds of Coriolanus
Should not be uttered feebly. It is held
That valour is the chiefest virtue, and
Most dignifies the haver. If it be,
The man I speak of cannot in the world
Be singly counterpoised. At sixteen years,
When Tarquin made a head for Rome, he fought
Beyond the mark of others; our then Dictator,
Whom with all praise I point at, saw him fight,
When with his Amazonian chin he drove
The bristled lips before him; he bestrid
An overpressed Roman and in the consul's view
Slew three opposers; Tarquin's self he met,
And struck him on his knee: in that day's feats,
When he might act the woman in the scene,
He proved best man in the field, and for his meed
Was brow-bound with the oak. His pupil age
Man-entered thus, he waxed like a sea;
And in the brunt of seventeen battles since
He lurched all swords of the garland. For this last,
Before and in Corioli, let me say,
I cannot speak him home. He stopped the fliers,
And by his rare example made the coward
Turn terror into sport; as weeds before
A vessel under sail, so men obeyed,
And fell below his stem. His sword, death's stamp,
Where it did mark, it took; from face to foot
He was a thing of blood, whose every motion

Was timed with dying cries. Alone he entered
The mortal gate of the city, which he painted
With shunless destiny; aidless came off,
And with a sudden re-enforcement struck
Corioli like a planet. Now all's his.
When, by and by the din of war 'gan pierce
His ready sense; then straight his doubled spirit
Re-quickened what in flesh was fatigate,
And to the battle came he; where he did
Run reeking over the lives of men, as if
'Twere a perpetual spoil; and till we called
Both field and city ours he never stood
To ease his breast with panting.

Coriolanus, Act 2 Scene 2
William Shakespeare (1564–1616)

The Crossing of the Rubicon

Caesar has crossed the Alps, his mighty soul great tumults pondering and the coming shock. Now on the marge of Rubicon, he saw, in face most sorrowful and ghostly guise, his trembling country's image; huge it seemed through mists of night obscure; and hoary hair streamed from the lofty front with turrets crowned: torn were her locks and naked were her arms. Then thus, with broken sighs the Vision spake: 'What seek ye, men of Rome? and whither hence bear ye my standards? If by right ye come, my citizens, stay here; these are the bounds; no further dare.' But Caesar's hair was stiff with horror as he gazed, and ghastly dread restrained his footsteps on the further bank. Then spake he, 'Thunderer, who from the rock Tarpeian seest the wall of mighty Rome; Gods of my race who watched over Troy of old; thou Jove of Alba's height, and vestal fires, and rites of Romulus erst rapt to heaven, and God-like Rome; be friendly to my quest. Not with offence or hostile arms I come, thy Caesar, conqueror by land and sea, thy soldier here and wheresoever thou wilt: No other's; his, his only be the guilt whose acts make me thy foe.' He gives the word and bids his standards cross the swollen stream. So in the wastes of Africa's burning clime the lion crouches as his foes draw near, feeding his wrath the while, his lashing tail provokes his fury; stiff upon his neck bristles his mane: deep from his gaping jaws resounds a muttered growl, and should a lance or javelin reach him from the hunter's ring, scorning the puny scratch he bounds afield.

From modest fountain blood-red Rubicon in summer's heat flows on; his pigmy tide creeps through the valleys and

with slender marge divides the Italian peasant from the gaul.
Then winter gave him strength, and fraught with rain the
third day's crescent moon; while eastern winds thawed from
the Alpine slopes the yielding snow. The cavalry first form
across the stream to break the torrent's force; the rest with
ease beneath their shelter gain the further bank. When
Caesar crossed and trod beneath his feet the soil of Italy's
forbidden fields, 'Here,' spake he, 'peace, here broken laws
be left; farewell to treaties. Fortune, lead me on; war is our
judge, and in the fates our trust.' Then in the shades of night
he leads the troops swifter than Balearic sling or shaft
winged by retreating Parthian, to the walls of threatened
Rimini, while fled the stars, save Lucifer, before the coming
sun, whose fires were veiled in clouds, by south wind driven,
or else at heaven's command: and thus drew on the first
dark morning of the civil war.

Pharsalia (*The Civil War*)
Lucan (AD39–65)
Translated by Sir Edward Ridley

The Last Fight of the *Revenge*

All the powder of the *Revenge* to the last barrel was now spent, all her pikes broken, forty of her best men slain, and the most part of the rest hurt. In the beginning of the fight she had but one hundred free from sickness, and fourscore and ten sick, laid in hold upon the ballast. A small troop to man such a ship, and a weak garrison to resist so mighty an army. By those hundred all was sustained, the volleys, boardings, and enterings of fifteen ships of war, besides those which beat her at large. On the contrary, the Spanish were always supplied with soldiers brought from every squadron: all manner of arms and powder at will. Unto ours there remained no comfort at all, no hope, no supply either of ships, men, or weapons; the masts all beaten overboard, all her tackle cut a sunder, her upper work altogether raised, and in effect evened she was with the water, but the very foundation or bottom of a ship, nothing being left overhead either for flight or defence. Sir Richard finding himself in this distress, and unable any longer to make resistance, having endured in this fifteen hours' fight, the assault of fifteen several Armadoes, all by turns aboard him, and by estimation eight hundred shot of great artillery, besides many assaults and entries; and that himself and the ship must needs be possessed by the enemy, who were now all cast in a ring about him; the *Revenge* not able to move one way or other, but as she was moved with the waves and billow of the sea: commanded the master Gunner, whom he knew to be a most resolute man, to split and sink the ship; that thereby nothing might remain of glory or victory to the Spaniards, seeing in so many hours' fight, and with so great a Navy they were not able to take her, having had fifteen hours' time, fifteen thousand men, and fifty and three sail of men-of-war to perform it withal: and persuaded the company, or as many as he could induce, to yield themselves unto God, and to the mercy of none else; but as they had like valiant resolute men, repulsed so many enemies, they should not now shorten the honour of their nation, by prolonging their own lives for a few hours, or a few days. The master Gunner readily condescended, and diverse others; but the Captain and the Master were of another opinion, and besought Sir Richard to have care of them: alleging that the Spaniard would be as ready to entertain a composition as they were willing to offer the same: and that there being diverse sufficient and valiant men yet living, and whose wounds were not mortal, they might do their country and prince acceptable service hereafter. And (that where Sir Richard had alleged that the Spaniards should never glory to have taken one ship of Her Majesty's seeing they had so long and so notably defended themselves) they answered, that the ship had six foot of water in hold, three shot under water, which were so weakly stopped as with the first working of the sea she must needs sink, and was besides so crushed and bruised as she could never be removed out of the place.

And as the matter was thus in dispute, and Sir Richard refusing to hearken to any of those reasons, the master of the *Revenge* (while the Captain wan unto him the greater party) was convoyed aboard the General, Don Alfonso Bassan. Who finding none over hasty to enter the *Revenge* again, doubting least Sir Richard would have blown them up and himself, and perceiving by the report of the master of the *Revenge* his dangerous disposition: yielded that all their lives should be saved, the company sent for England, and the better sort to pay such reasonable ransom as their estate would bear, and in the mean season to be free from galley or imprisonment. To this he so much the rather condescended as well as I have said, for fear of further loss and mischief to themselves, as also for the desire he had to recover Sir Richard Grenville; whom for his notable valour he seemed greatly to honour and admire.

A Report of the Truth of the Fight about
the Isle of Azores betwixt the Revenge and an
Armada of the King of Spain
Sir Walter Raleigh (1554–1618)

Clive at Plassey
A Nineteenth-Century Account

Clive was in a painfully anxious situation. He could place no confidence in the sincerity or in the courage of his confederate: and, whatever confidence he might place in his own military talents, and in the valour and discipline of his troops, it was no light thing to engage an army twenty times numerous as his own. Before him lay a river over which it was easy to advance, but over which, if things went ill, not one of his little band would ever return. On this occasion, for the first and for the last time, his dauntless spirit, during a few hours, shrank from the fearful responsibility of making a decision. He called a council of war. The majority pronounced against fighting; and Clive declared his concurrence with the majority. Long afterwards, he said that he had never called but one council of war, and that, if he had taken the advice of that council, the British would never have been masters of Bengal. But scarcely had the meeting broken up when he was himself again. He retired alone under the shade of some trees, and passed near an hour there in thought. He came back determined to put everything to the hazard, and gave orders that all should be in readiness for passing the river on the morrow.

The river was passed; and, at the close of a toilsome day's march, the army, long after sunset, took up its quarters in grove of mango trees near Plassey, within a mile of the enemy. Clive was unable to sleep; he heard, through the whole night, the sound of drums and cymbals from the vast camp of the Nabob. It is not strange that even his stout heart should now and then have sunk, when he reflected against what odds, and for what a prize, he was in a few hours to contend.

Nor was the rest of Surajah Dowlah more peaceful. His mind, at once weak and stormy, was distracted by wild and horrible apprehensions. Appalled by the greatness and nearness of the crisis, distrusting his captains, dreading every one who approached him, dreading to be left alone, he sat gloomily in his tent, haunted, a Greek poet would have said, by the furies of those who had cursed him with their last breath in the Black Hole.

The day broke, the day which was to decide the fate of India. At sunrise the army of the Nabob, pouring through many openings from the camp, began to move towards the grove where the English lay. Forty thousand infantry, armed with firelocks, pikes, swords, bows and arrows, covered the plain. They were accompanied by fifty pieces of ordnance of the largest size, each tugged by a long team of white oxen, and each pushed on from behind by an elephant. Some smaller guns, under the direction of a few French auxiliaries, were perhaps more formidable. The cavalry were fifteen thousand, drawn, not from the effeminate population of Bengal, but from the bolder race which inhabits the northern provinces; and the practised eye of Clive could perceive that both the men and the horses were more powerful than those of the Carnatic. The force which he had to oppose to this great multitude consisted of only three thousand men. But of these nearly a thousand were English; and all were led by English officers, and trained in the English discipline. Conspicuous in the ranks of the little army were the men of the Thirty-Ninth Regiment, which still bears on its colours, amidst many honourable additions won under Wellington in Spain and Gascony, the name of Plassey, and the proud motto, *Primus in Indis*.

The battle commenced with a cannonade in which the artillery of the Nabob did scarcely any execution, while the few field-pieces of the English produced great effect. Several of the most distinguished officers in Surajah Dowlah's service fell. Disorder began to spread through his ranks. His own terror increased every moment. One of the conspirators urged on him the expediency of retreating. The insidious advice, agreeing as it did with what his own terrors suggested, was readily received. He ordered his army to fall back, and this order decided his fate. Clive snatched the moment, and ordered his troops to advance. The confused and dispirited multitude gave way before the onset of disciplined valour. No mob attacked by regular soldiers was ever more completely routed. The little band of Frenchmen, who alone ventured to confront the English, were swept down the stream of fugitives. In an hour the forces of Surajah Dowlah were dispersed, never to reassemble. Only five hundred of the vanquished were slain. But their camp, their guns, their baggage, innumerable wagons, innumerable cattle, remained in the power of the conquerors. With the loss of twenty-two soldiers killed and fifty wounded, Clive had scattered an army of near sixty thousand men, and subdued an empire larger and more populous than Great Britain.

Essays
Thomas Babington, Lord Macaulay (1800–59)

The True Knight

For knighthood is not in the feats of war,
As for to fight in quarrel right or wrong,
But in a cause which truth can not defar:
   He ought himself for to make sure and strong,
   Justice to keep mixt with mercy among:
      And no quarrel a knight ought to take
      But for a truth, or for the common's sake.

Stephen Hawes (*c.* 1475–1511)

Wartime

Grotesque

These are the damned circles Dante trod,
Terrible in hopelessness,
But even skulls have their humour,
An eyeless and sardonic mockery:
And we,
Sitting with streaming eyes in the acrid smoke,
That murks our foul, damp billet,
Chant bitterly, with raucous voices
As a choir of frogs
In hideous irony, our patriotic songs.

Frederic Manning (1882–1935)

The Battle of Blenheim

It was a summer evening,
    Old Kaspar's work was done,
And he before his cottage door
    Was sitting in the sun,
And by him sported on the green
His little grandchild Wilhelmine.

She saw her brother Peterkin
    Roll something large and round
Which he beside the rivulet
    In playing there had found;
He came to ask what he had found,
That was so large, and smooth, and round.

Old Kaspar took it from the boy,
    Who stood expectant by;
And then the old man shook his head,
    And with a natural sigh,
''Tis some poor fellow's skull,' said he,
'Who fell in the great victory.

'I find them in the garden,
    For there's many here about;
And often when I go to plough,
    The ploughshare turns them out!
For many thousand men,' said he,
'Were slain in that great victory.'

'Now tell us what 'twas all about,'
    Young Peterkin, he cries;
And little Wilhelmine looks up
    With wonder-waiting eyes;
'Now tell us all about the war,
And what they fought each other for.'

'It was the English,' Kaspar cried,
    'Who put the French to rout;
But what they fought each other for
    I could not well make out;
But everybody said,' quoth he,
'That 'twas a famous victory.

'My father lived at Blenheim then,
    Yon little stream hard by;
They burnt his dwelling to the ground,
    And he was forced to fly;
So with his wife and child he fled,
Nor had he where to rest his head.

'With fire and sword the country round
    Was wasted far and wide,
And many a childing mother then,
    And new-born baby died;
But things like that, you know, must be
At every famous victory.

'They said it was a shocking sight
    After the field was won;
For many thousand bodies here

Lay rotting in the sun;
But things like that, you know, must be
After a famous victory.

'Great praise the Duke of Marlbro' won,
    And our good Prince Eugene.'
'Why, 'twas a very wicked thing!'
    Said little Wilhelmine.
'Nay ... nay ... my little girl,' quoth he,
'It was a famous victory.'

'And everybody praised the Duke
    Who this great fight did win.'
'But what good came of it at last?'
    Quoth little Peterkin.
'Why, that I cannot tell,' said he,
'But 'twas a famous victory.'

Robert Southey (1774–1843)

The Contention of Ajax and Ulysses

The glories of our blood and state
  Are shadows, not substantial things;
There is no armour against fate;
  Death lays his icy hand on kings;
        Sceptre and Crown
        Must tumble down,
And in the dust be equal made
With the poor crooked scythe and spade.

Some men with swords may reap the field,
  And plant fresh laurels where they kill;
But their strong nerves at last must yield;
  They tame but one another still.
        Early or late,
        They stoop to fate,
And must give up their murmuring breath
When they, pale captives, creep to death.

The garlands wither on your brow;
  Then boast no more your mighty deeds.
Upon Death's purple altar now,
  See where the victor-victim bleeds.
        Your heads must come
        To the cold tomb.
Only the actions of the just
Smell sweet, and blossom in their dust.

James Shirley (1596–1666)

Attack on the Trojan Camp

And now the trumpets terribly from far,
With rattling clangour, rouse the sleepy war.
The soldiers' shouts succeed the brazen sounds;
And heaven, from pole to pole, the noise rebounds.
The Volscians bear their shields upon their head,
And, rushing forward, form a moving shed.
These fill the ditch; those pull the bulwarks down:
Some raise the ladders; others scale the town.
But, where void spaces on the walls appear,
Or thin defence, they pour their forces there.
With poles and missive weapons, from afar,
The Trojans keep aloof the rising war.
Taught, by their ten years' siege, defensive fight,
They roll down ribs of rocks, an unresisted weight,
To break the penthouse with the ponderous blow,
Which yet the patient Volscians undergo:
But could not bear the unequal combat long;
For, where the Trojans find the thickest throng,
The ruin falls: their shattered shields give way,
And their crushed heads become an easy prey.
They shrink for fear, abated of their rage,
Nor longer dare in a blind fight engage;
Contented now to gall them from below
With darts and slings, and with the distant bow.

The Aeneid, Book IX
Virgil (70–19 BC)
Translated by John Dryden (1631–1700)

The Lesson of the War

The feast is spread through England
    For rich and poor today;
Greetings and laughter may be there,
    But thoughts are far away;
Over the stormy ocean,
    Over the dreary track,
Where some are gone, whom England
    Will never welcome back.

Breathless she waits, and listens
    For every eastern breeze
That bears upon its bloody wings
    News from beyond the seas.
The leafless branches stirring
    Make many a watcher start;
The distant tramp of steed may send
    A throb from heart to heart.

The rulers of the nation,
    The poor ones at their gate,
With the same eager wonder
    The same great news await.
The poor man's stay and comfort,
    The rich man's joy and pride,
Upon the bleak Crimean shore
    Are fighting side by side.

The bullet comes – and either
    A desolate hearth may see;

And God alone tonight knows where
   The vacant place may be!
The dread that stirs the peasant
   Thrills nobles' hearts with fear –
Yet above selfish sorrow
   Both hold their country dear.

The rich man who reposes
   In his ancestral shade,
The peasant at his ploughshare,
   The worker at his trade,
Each one his all has perilled,
   Each has the same great stake,
Each soul can but have patience,
   Each heart can only break!

Hushed is all party clamour;
   One thought in every heart,
One dread in every household,
   Has bid such strife depart.
England has called her children;
   Long silent – the word came
That lit the smouldering ashes
   Through all the land to flame.

Oh you who toil and suffer,
   You gladly heard the call;
But those you sometimes envy
   Have they not given their all?
Oh you who rule the nation,
   Take now the toil-worn hand –

Brothers you are in sorrow,
  In duty to your land.
Learn but this noble lesson
  Ere Peace returns again,
And the life-blood of Old England
  Will not be shed in vain.

Adelaide Anne Procter (1825–64)

Retort on the Foregoing

I hate that drum's discordant sound,
Parading round, and round, and round:
To thoughtless youth it pleasure yields,
And lures from cities and from fields,
To sell their liberty for charms
Of tawdry lace, and glittering arms;
And when Ambition's voice commands,
To march, and fight, and fall, in foreign lands.

I hate that drum's discordant sound,
Parading round, and round, and round:
To me it talks of ravaged plains,
And burning towns, and ruined swains,
And mangled limbs, and dying groans,
And widows' tears, and orphans' moans;
And all that Misery's hand bestows,
To fill the catalogue of human woes.

John Scott of Amwell (1730–83)

The Going of the Battery
Wives' Lament (2 November 1899)

I

O it was sad enough, weak enough, mad enough –
Light in their loving as soldiers can be –
First to risk choosing them, leave alone losing them
Now, in far battle, beyond the south sea! ...

II

– Rain came down drenchingly; but we unblenchingly
Trudged on beside them through murk and through mire,
They stepping steadily – only too readily! –
Scarce as if stepping brought parting time nigher.

III

Great guns were gleaming there, living things seeming there,
Cloaked in their tar cloths, upmouthed to the night;
Wheels wet and yellow from axle to felloe,
Throats blank of sound, but prophetic to sight.

IV

Gas glimmers drearily, blearily, eerily
Lit our pale faces outstretched for one kiss,
While we stood prest to them, with a last quest to them
Not to court perils that honour could miss.

V

Sharp were those sighs of ours, blinded these eyes of ours,
When at last moved away under the arch

All we loved. Aid for them each woman prayed for them,
Treading back slowly the track of their march.

VI

Someone said: 'Nevermore will they come: evermore
Are they now lost to us.' O it was wrong!
Though may be hard their ways, some hand will guard
their ways,
Bear them through safely, in brief time or long.

VII

– Yet, voices haunting us, daunting us, taunting us,
Hint in the night time when life beats are low
Other and graver things ... Hold we to braver things,
Wait we, in trust, what time's fullness shall show.

Thomas Hardy (1840–1928)

The Send-Off

Down the close darkening lanes they sang their way
To the siding-shed,
And lined the train with faces grimly gay.

Their breasts were stuck all white with wreath and spray
As men's are, dead.

Dull porters watched them, and a casual tramp
Stood staring hard,
Sorry to miss them from the upland camp.

Then, unmoved, signals nodded, and a lamp
Winked to the guard.

So secretly, like wrongs hushed-up, they went.
They were not ours:
We never heard to which front these were sent.

Nor there if they yet mock what women meant
Who gave them flowers.

Shall they return to beatings of great bells
In wild train-loads?
A few, a few, too few for drums and yells,

May creep back, silent, to village wells
Up half-known roads.

Wilfred Owen (1893–1918)

A March in the Ranks Hard-Prest, and the Road Unknown

A march in the ranks hard-prest, and the road unknown,
A route through a heavy wood with muffled steps in the darkness,
Our army foiled with loss severe, and the sullen remnant retreating,
Till after midnight glimmer upon us the lights of a dim-lighted
    building,
We come to an open space in the woods, and halt by the dim-
    lighted building,
'Tis a large old church at the crossing roads, now an impromptu
    hospital,
Entering but for a minute I see a sight beyond all the pictures
    and poems ever made,
Shadows of deepest, deepest black, just lit by moving candles and
    lamps,
And by one great pitchy torch stationary with wild red flame and
    clouds of smoke,
By these, crowds, groups of forms vaguely I see on the floor,
    some in the pews laid down,
At my feet more distinctly a soldier, a mere lad, in danger of
    bleeding to death, (he is shot in the abdomen)
I stanch the blood temporarily, (the youngster's face is white as
    a lily)
Then before I depart I sweep my eyes o'er the scene fain to
    absorb it all,
Faces, varieties, postures beyond description, most in obscurity,
    some of them dead,
Surgeons operating, attendants holding lights, the smell of ether,
    odour of blood,
The crowd, O the crowd of the bloody forms, the yard outside
    also filled,

Some on the bare ground, some on planks or stretchers, some in
   the death-spasm sweating,
An occasional scream or cry, the doctor's shouted orders or calls,
The glisten of the little steel instruments catching the glint of the
   torches,
These I resume as I chant, I see again the forms, I smell the odour,
Then hear outside the orders given, *Fall in, my men, fall in*;
But first I bend to the dying lad, his eyes open, a half-smile gives
   he me,
Then the eyes close, calmly close, and I speed forth to the darkness,
Resuming, marching, ever in darkness marching, on in the ranks,
The unknown road still marching.

Walt Whitman (1819–92)

The Bivouac in the Snow

Halt! – the march is over,
    Day is almost done;
Loose the cumbrous knapsack,
    Drop the heavy gun.
Chilled and wet and weary,
    Wander to and fro,
Seeking wood to kindle
    Fires amidst the snow.

Round the bright blaze gather,
    Heed not sleet or cold;
Ye are Spartan soldiers,
    Stout and brave and bold.
Never Xerxian army
    Yet subdued a foe
Who but asked a blanket
    On a bed of snow.

Shivering, 'midst the darkness,
    Christian men are found,
There devoutly kneeling
    On the frozen ground –
Pleading for their country,
    In its hour of woe –
For the soldiers marching
    Shoeless through the snow.

Lost in heavy slumbers,
  Free from toil and strife,
Dreaming of their dear ones –
  Home, and child, and wife –
Tentless they are lying,
  While the fires burn low –
Lying in their blankets
  'Midst December's snow.

Margaret Junkin Preston (1820–97)

Bivouac on a Mountain Side

I see before me now a travelling army halting,
Below a fertile valley spread, with barns and the orchards
  of summer,
Behind, the terraced sides of a mountain, abrupt, in places
  rising high,
Broken, with rocks, with clinging cedars, with tall shapes
  dingily seen,
The numerous camp fires scattered near and far, some
  away up on the mountain,
The shadowy forms of men and horses, looming, large-sized,
  flickering,
And all over the sky – the sky! far, far out of reach, studded,
  breaking out, the eternal stars.

Walt Whitman (1819–92)

Exposure

Our brains ache, in the merciless iced east winds that knife us ...
Wearied we keep awake because the night is silent ...
Low, drooping flares confuse our memory of the salient ...
Worried by silence, sentries whisper, curious, nervous,
    But nothing happens.

Watching, we hear the mad gusts tugging on the wire,
Like twitching agonies of men among its brambles.
Northward, incessantly, the flickering gunnery rumbles,
Far off, like a dull rumour of some other war.
    What are we doing here?

The poignant misery of dawn begins to grow ...
We only know war lasts, rain soaks, and clouds sag stormy.
Dawn massing in the east her melancholy army
Attacks once more in ranks on shivering ranks of grey,
    But nothing happens.

Sudden successive flights of bullets streak the silence.
Less deadly than the air that shudders black with snow,
With sidelong flowing flakes that flock, pause and renew;
We watch them wandering up and down the wind's nonchalance,
    But nothing happens.

Pale flakes with lingering stealth come feeling for our faces –
We cringe in holes, back on forgotten dreams, and stare, snow-dazed,
Deep into grassier ditches. So we drowse, sun-dozed,
Littered with blossoms trickling where the blackbird fusses,
    – Is it that we are dying?

Slowly our ghosts drag home: glimpsing the sunk fires, glozed
With crusted dark-red jewels; crickets jingle there;
For hours the innocent mice rejoice: the house is theirs;
Shutters and doors all closed: on us the doors are closed, –
    We turn back to our dying.

Since we believe not otherwise can kind fires burn;
Now ever suns smile true on child, or field, or fruit.
For God's invincible spring our love is made afraid;
Therefore, not loath, we lie out here; therefore were born,
    For love of God seems dying.

Tonight, His frost will fasten on this mud and us,
Shrivelling many hands and puckering foreheads crisp.
The burying party, picks and shovels in their shaking grasp,
Pause over half-known faces. All their eyes are ice,
    But nothing happens.

                    Wilfred Owen (1893–1918)

Break of Day in the Trenches

The darkness crumbles away.
It is the same old druid Time as ever,
Only a live thing leaps my hand,
A queer sardonic rat,
As I pull the parapet's poppy
To stick behind my ear.
Droll rat, they would shoot you if they knew
Your cosmopolitan sympathies.
Now you have touched this English hand
You will do the same to a German
Soon, no doubt, if it be your pleasure
To cross the sleeping green between.
It seems you inwardly grin as you pass
Strong eyes, fine limbs, haughty athletes
Less chanced than you for life,
Bonds to the whims of murder,
Sprawled in the bowels of the earth,
The torn fields of France.
What do you see in our eyes
At the shrieking iron and flame
Hurled through still heavens?
What quaver – what heart aghast?
Poppies whose roots are in man's veins
Drop, and are ever dropping;
But mine in my ear is safe –
Just a little white with the dust.

Isaac Rosenberg (1890–1918)

The Immortals

I killed them, but they would not die.
Yea! All the day and all the night
For them I could not rest nor sleep,
Nor guard from them nor hide in flight.

Then in my agony I turned
And made my hands red in their gore.
In vain – for faster than I slew
They rose more cruel than before.

I killed and killed with slaughter mad;
I killed till all my strength was gone.
And still they rose to torture me,
For Devils only die for fun.

I used to think the Devil hid
In women's smiles and wine's carouse.
I called him Satan, Balzebub.
But now I call him dirty louse.

Isaac Rosenberg (1890–1918)

Desertion

So light we were, so right we were, so fair faith shone,
And the way was laid so certainly, that, when I'd gone,
What dumb thing looked up at you? Was it something heard,
Or a sudden cry, that meekly and without a word
You broke the faith, and strangely, weakly, slipped apart.
You gave in – you, the proud of heart, unbowed of heart!
Was this, friend, the end of all that we could do?
And have you found the best for you, the rest for you?
Did you learn so suddenly (and I not by!)
Some whispered story, that stole the glory from the sky,
And ended all the splendid dream, and made you go
So dully from the fight we know, the light we know?

O faithless! the faith remains, and I must pass
Gay down the way, and on alone. Under the grass
You wait; the breeze moves in the trees, and stirs, and calls,
And covers you with white petals, with light petals.
There it shall crumble, frail and fair, under the sun,
O little heart, your brittle heart; till day be done,
And the shadows gather, falling light, and, white with dew,
Whisper, and weep; and creep to you. Good sleep to you!

Rupert Brooke (1887–1915)

Smile, Smile, Smile
23 September 1918

Head to limp head, the sunk-eyed wounded scanned
Yesterday's *Mail*; the casualties (typed small)
And (large) Vast Booty from our Latest Haul.
Also, they read of Cheap Homes, not yet planned;
For, said the paper, When this war is done
The men's first instincts will be making homes.
Meanwhile their foremost need is aerodromes,
It being certain war has but begun.
Peace would do wrong to our undying dead, –
The sons we offered might regret they died
If we got nothing lasting in their stead.
We must be solidly indemnified.
Though all be worthy Victory which all bought,
We rulers sitting in this ancient spot
Would wrong our very selves if we forgot
The greatest glory will be theirs who fought,
Who kept this nation in integrity.
Nation? – The half-limbed readers did not chafe
But smiled at one another curiously
Like secret men who know their secret safe.
(This is the thing they know and never speak,
That England one by one had fled to France,
Not many elsewhere now, save under France.)
Pictures of these broad smiles appear each week,
And people in whose voice real feeling rings
Say: How they smile! They're happy now, poor things.

Wilfred Owen (1893–1918)

Channel Firing

That night your great guns, unawares,
Shook all our coffins as we lay,
And broke the chancel window squares,
We thought it was the Judgment day

And sat upright. While drearisome
Arose the howl of wakened hounds:
The mouse let fall the altar crumb,
The worm drew back into the mounds,

The glebe cow drooled. Till God cried, 'No;
It's gunnery practice out at sea
Just as before you went below;
The world is as it used to be:

'All nations striving strong to make
Red war yet redder. Mad as hatters
They do no more for Christés sake
Than you who are helpless in such matters.

'That this is not the judgment-hour
For some of them's a blessed thing,
For if it were they'd have to scour
Hell's floor for so much threatening ...

'Ha, ha. It will be warmer when
I blow the trumpet (if indeed
I ever do; for you are men,
And rest eternal sorely need).'

So down we lay again. 'I wonder,
Will the world ever saner be,'
Said one, 'than when He sent us under
In our indifferent century!'

And many a skeleton shook his head.
'Instead of preaching forty year,'
My neighbour Parson Thirdly said,
'I wish I had stuck to pipes and beer.'

Again the guns disturbed the hour,
Roaring their readiness to avenge,
As far inland as Stourton Tower,
And Camelot, and starlit Stonehenge.

Thomas Hardy (1840–1928)

On Receiving News of the War

Snow is a strange white word.
No ice or frost
Has asked of bud or bird
For winter's cost.

Yet ice and frost and snow
From earth to sky
This summer land doth know.
No man knows why.

In all men's hearts it is.
Some spirit old
Hath turned with malign kiss
Our lives to mould.

Red fangs have torn His face.
God's blood is shed.
He mourns from His lone place
His children dead.

O! ancient crimson curse!
Corrode, consume.
Give back this universe
Its pristine bloom.

Isaac Rosenberg (1890–1918)

Death or Glory?

Stanzas

When a man hath no freedom to fight for at home,
    Let him combat for that of his neighbours;
Let him think of the glories of Greece and of Rome,
    And get knocked on the head for his labours.

To do good to mankind is the chivalrous plan,
    And is always as nobly requited;
Then battle for freedom wherever you can,
    And, if not shot or hanged, you'll get knighted.

George Gordon, Lord Byron (1788–1824)

Breathes There the Man

Breathes there the man, with soul so dead,
Who never to himself hath said,
   This is my own, my native land!
Whose heart hath ne'er within him burned,
As home his footsteps he hath turned,
   From wandering on a foreign strand!
If such there breathe, go, mark him well;
For him no minstrel raptures swell;
High though his titles, proud his name,
Boundless his wealth as wish can claim;
Despite those titles, power, and pelf,
The wretch, concentred all in self,
Living, shall forfeit fair renown,
And, doubly dying, shall go down
To the vile dust, from whence he sprung,
Unwept, unhonoured, and unsung.

The Lay of the Last Minstrel
Sir Walter Scott (1771–1832)

Volunteer's Song, Written in 1803

Ye who Britain's soldiers be, –
Freemen, children of the free,
Who quickly come at danger's call,
From shop and palace, cot and hall,
And brace ye bravely up in warlike gear,
       For all that ye hold dear;

Blest in your hands be sword and spear!
There is no banded Briton here
On whom some fond mate hath not smiled,
Or hung in love some lisping child,
Or aged parent, grasping his last stay,
       With locks of honoured gray

Such men behold with steady pride,
The threatened tempest gathering wide,
And list with onward form inclined
To sound of foe-men on the wind,
And bravely act amid the battle's roar,
       In scenes untried before.

Let veterans boast, as well they may,
Nerves steeled in many a bloody day;
The generous heart, who takes his stand
Upon his free and native land,
Doth, with the first sound of the hostile drum,
       A fearless man become.

Then come, ye hosts, that madly pour
From wave-tossed floats upon our shore!
If fell or gentle, false or true,
Let those inquire, who wish to sue:
Nor fiend nor hero from a foreign strand,
   Shall lord it in our land.

Come, then, ye hosts that madly pour
From wave-tossed floats upon our shore!
An adverse wind or breezeless main
Locked in their ports our tars detain,
To waste their eager spirits, vainly keen,
   Else here ye had not been.

Yet ne'ertheless, in strong array,
Prepare ye for a well-fought day.
Let banners wave and trumpets sound,
And closing cohorts darken round,
And the fierce onset raise its mingled roar,
   New sound on England's shore!

Freemen, children of the free,
Are brave alike on land or sea;
And every rood of British ground
On which a hostile spear is found,
Proves under their firm tread and vigorous stroke,
   A deck of royal oak.

      Joanna Baillie (1762–1851)

The Soldier

If I should die, think only this of me:
    That there's some corner of a foreign field
That is for ever England. There shall be
    In that rich earth a richer dust concealed;
A dust whom England bore, shaped, made aware,
    Gave, once, her flowers to love, her ways to roam,
A body of England's, breathing English air,
    Washed by the rivers, blest by suns of home.

And think, this heart, all evil shed away,
    A pulse in the eternal mind, no less
        Gives somewhere back the thoughts by England given;
Her sights and sounds; dreams happy as her day;
    And laughter, learnt of friends; and gentleness,
        In hearts at peace, under an English heaven.

Rupert Brooke (1887–1915)

Say Not the Struggle Naught Availeth

Say not the struggle naught availeth,
The labour and the wounds are vain,
The enemy faints not, nor faileth,
And as things have been they remain.

If hopes were dupes, fears may be liars;
It may be, in yon smoke concealed,
Your comrades chase e'en now the fliers,
And, but for you, possess the field.

For while the tired waves, vainly breaking,
Seem here no painful inch to gain,
Far back, through creeks and inlets making,
Comes silent, flooding in, the main.

And not by eastern windows only,
When daylight comes, comes in the light;
In front the sun climbs slow, how slowly,
But westward, look, the land is bright!

Arthur Hugh Clough (1819–61)

Battle Hymn of the American Republic

Mine eyes have seen the glory of the coming of the Lord;
He is trampling out the vintage where the grapes of wrath are stored;
He hath loosed the fateful lightning of his terrible swift sword:
 His Truth is marching on.

I have seen him in the watch fires of a hundred circling camps;
They have builded him an altar in the evening dews and damps;
I have read his righteous sentence by the dim and flaring lamps:
 His Day is marching on.

I have read a fiery gospel, writ in burnished rows of steel:
'As you deal with my contemners, so with you my grace shall deal;'
Let the hero born of woman crush the serpent with his heel,
 Since God is marching on.

He has sounded forth the trumpet that shall never call retreat;
He is sifting out the hearts of men before his judgment seat;
O be swift, my soul, to answer him; be jubilant, my feet!
 Our God is marching on.

In the beauty of the lilies Christ was born across the sea,
With a glory in his bosom that transfigures you and me;
As he died to make men holy, let us die to make men free,
 While God is marching on.

He is coming like the glory of the morning on the wave;
He is wisdom to the mighty, he is succour to the brave;
So the world shall be his footstool, and the soul of time his slave,
 Our God is marching on.

Julia Ward Howe (1819–1910)

Scots Wha Hae

Scots, wha hae wi' Wallace bled,
Scots, wham Bruce has aften led,
Welcome to your gory bed,
Or to victorie.

Now's the day, and now's the hour,
See the front o' battle lour!
See approach proud Edward's power –
Chains and slaverie!

Wha will be a traitor knave?
Wha can fill a coward's grave?
Wha sae base as be a slave?
Let him turn and flee!

Wha for Scotland's king and law
Freedom's sword will strongly draw,
Freeman stand, or freeman fa'?
Let him follow me!

By oppression's woes and pains,
By your sons in servile chains!
We will drain our dearest veins,
But they shall be free!

Lay the proud usurpers low!
Tyrants fall in every foe!
Liberty's in every blow!
Let us do or die!

Robert Burns (1759–96)

Ye Mariners of England

Ye Mariners of England
   That guard our native seas!
Whose flag has braved a thousand years,
   The battle and the breeze!
Your glorious standard launch again
   To match another foe;
And sweep through the deep,
   While the stormy winds do blow!
While the battle rages loud and long,
   And the stormy winds do blow.

The spirits of your fathers
   Shall start from every wave –
For the deck it was their field of fame,
   And ocean was their grave:
Where Blake and mighty Nelson fell
   Your manly hearts shall glow,
As ye sweep through the deep,
   While the stormy winds do blow!
While the battle rages loud and long,
   And the stormy winds do blow.

Britannia needs no bulwarks,
   No towers along the steep;
Her march is o'er the mountain waves,
   Her home is on the deep.
With thunders from her native oak
   She quells the floods below,
As they roar on the shore,

When the stormy winds do blow!
When the battle rages loud and long,
  And the stormy winds do blow.

The meteor flag of England
  Shall yet terrific burn;
Till danger's troubled night depart
  And the star of peace return.
Then, then, ye ocean warriors!
  Our song and feast shall flow
To the fame of your name,
  When the storm has ceased to blow!
When the fiery fight is heard no more,
  And the storm has ceased to blow.

Thomas Campbell (1777–1844)

The Destruction of Sennacherib

The Assyrian came down like the wolf on the fold,
And his cohorts were gleaming in purple and gold;
And the sheen of their spears was like stars on the sea,
When the blue wave rolls nightly on deep Galilee.

Like the leaves of the forest when summer is green,
That host with their banners at sunset were seen:
Like the leaves of the forest when autumn hath blown,
That host on the morrow lay withered and strown.

For the Angel of Death spread his wings on the blast,
And breathed in the face of the foe as he passed;
And the eyes of the sleepers waxed deadly and chill,
And their hearts but once heaved, and for ever grew still!

And there lay the steed with his nostril all wide,
But through it there rolled not the breath of his pride:
And the foam of his gasping lay white on the turf,
And cold as the spray of the rock-beating surf.

And there lay the rider distorted and pale,
With the dew on his brow, and the rust on his mail;
And the tents were all silent, the banners alone,
The lances unlifted, the trumpet unblown.

And the widows of Ashur are loud in their wail,
And the idols are broke in the temple of Baal;
And the might of the gentile, unsmote by the sword,
Hath melted like snow in the glance of the Lord!

George Gordon, Lord Byron (1788–1824)

How They Brought the Good News from Ghent to Aix

I sprang to the stirrup, and Joris, and he;
I galloped, Dirck galloped, we galloped all three;
'Good speed!' cried the watch, as the gate-bolts undrew;
'Speed!' echoed the wall to us galloping through;
Behind shut the postern, the lights sank to rest,
And into the midnight we galloped abreast.

Not a word to each other; we kept the great pace
Neck by neck, stride by stride, never changing our place;
I turned in my saddle and made its girths tight,
Then shortened each stirrup, and set the pique right,
Rebuckled the cheek-strap, chained slacker the bit,
Nor galloped less steadily Roland a whit.

'Twas moonset at starting; but while we drew near
Lokeren, the cocks crew and twilight dawned clear;
At Boom, a great yellow star came out to see;
At Düffeld, 'twas morning as plain as could be;
And from Mecheln church-steeple we heard the half-chime,
So Joris broke silence with, 'Yet there is time!'

At Aerschot, up leaped of a sudden the sun,
And against him the cattle stood black every one,
To stare through the mist at us galloping past,
And I saw my stout galloper Roland at last,
With resolute shoulders, each butting away
The haze, as some bluff river headland its spray.

And his low head and crest, just one sharp ear bent back
For my voice, and the other pricked out on his track;
And one eye's black intelligence, – ever that glance
O'er its white edge at me, his own master, askance!
And the thick heavy spume-flakes which aye and anon
His fierce lips shook upwards in galloping on.

By Hasselt, Dirck groaned; and cried Joris, 'Stay spur!
Your Roos galloped bravely, the fault's not in her,
We'll remember at Aix' – for one heard the quick wheeze
Of her chest, saw the stretched neck and staggering knees,
And sunk tail, and horrible heave of the flank,
As down on her haunches she shuddered and sank.

So we were left galloping, Joris and I,
Past Looz and past Tongres, no cloud in the sky;
The broad sun above laughed a pitiless laugh,
'Neath our feet broke the brittle bright stubble like chaff;
Till over by Dalhem a dome-spire sprang white,
And 'Gallop,' gasped Joris, 'for Aix is in sight!'

'How they'll greet us!' – and all in a moment his roan
Rolled neck and croup over, lay dead as a stone;
And there was my Roland to bear the whole weight
Of the news which alone could save Aix from her fate,
With his nostrils like pits full of blood to the brim,
And with circles of red for his eye-sockets' rim.

Then I cast loose my buffcoat, each holster let fall,
Shook off both my jack-boots, let go belt and all,
Stood up in the stirrup, learned, patted his ear,

Called my Roland his pet-name, my horse without peer;
Clapped my hands, laughed and sang, any noise, bad or good,
Till at length into Aix Roland galloped and stood.

And all I remember is, friends flocking round
As I sat with his head 'twixt my knees on the ground;
And no voice but was praising this Roland of mine,
As I poured down his throat our last measure of wine,
Which (the burgesses voted by common consent)
Was no more than his due who brought good news from Ghent.

Robert Browning (1812–89)

Into Battle

The naked earth is warm with spring,
   And with green grass and bursting trees
Leans to the sun's gaze glorying,
   And quivers in the sunny breeze;

And life is colour and warmth and light,
   And a striving evermore for these;
And he is dead who will not fight;
   And who dies fighting has increase.

The fighting man shall from the sun
   Take warmth, and life from the glowing earth;
Speed with the light-foot winds to run,
   And with the trees to newer birth;
And find, when fighting shall be done,
   Great rest, and fullness after dearth.

All the bright company of heaven
   Hold him in their high comradeship,
The Dog-Star, and the Sisters Seven,
   Orion's Belt and sworded hip.

The woodland trees that stand together,
   They stand to him each one a friend;
They gently speak in the windy weather;
   They guide to valley and ridge's end.

The kestrel hovering by day,
   And the little owls that call by night,

Bid him be swift and keen as they,
  As keen of ear, as swift of sight.

The blackbird sings to him, 'Brother, brother,
  If this be the last song you shall sing,
Sing well, for you may not sing another;
  Brother, sing.'

In dreary, doubtful waiting hours,
  Before the brazen frenzy starts,
The horses show him nobler powers;
  O patient eyes, courageous hearts!

And when the burning moment breaks,
  And all things else are out of mind,
And only joy of battle takes
  Him by the throat, and makes him blind,

Through joy and blindness he shall know,
  Not caring much to know, that still
Nor lead nor steel shall reach him, so
  That it be not the Destined Will.

The thundering line of battle stands,
  And in the air Death moans and sings:
But Day shall clasp him with strong hands,
  And Night shall fold him in soft wings.

Julian Grenfell (1888–1915)

All the Hills and Vales Along

All the hills and vales along
Earth is bursting into song,
And the singers are the chaps
Who are going to die perhaps.
   O sing, marching men,
   Till the valleys ring again,
   Give your gladness to earth's keeping,
   So be glad, when you are sleeping.

Cast away regret and rue,
Think what you are marching to.
Little live, great pass.
Jesus Christ and Barabbas
Were found the same day.
This died, that went his way.
   So sing with joyful breath.
   For why, you are gong to death.
   Teeming earth will surely store
   All the gladness that you pour.

Earth that never doubts nor fears,
Earth that knows of death, not tears,
Earth that bore with joyful ease
Hemlock for Socrates,
Earth that blossomed and was glad
'Neath the cross that Christ had,
Shall rejoice and blossom too
When the bullet reaches you.
   Wherefore, men marching

On the road to death, sing!
Pour gladness on earth's head,
So be merry, so be dead.

From the hills and valleys earth
Shouts back the sound of mirth,
Tramp of feet and lilt of song
Ringing all the road along.
All the music of their going,
Ringing swinging glad song-throwing,
Earth will echo still, when foot
Lies numb and voice mute.
　　On marching men, on
　　To the gates of death with song.
　　Sow your gladness for earth's reaping,
　　So you may be glad, though sleeping.
　　Strew your gladness on earth's bed,
　　So be merry, so be dead.

Charles Hamilton Sorley (1895–1915)

The Last Buccanier

Oh England is a pleasant place for them that's rich and high,
But England is a cruel place for such poor folks as I;
And such a port for mariners I ne'er shall see again
As the pleasant Isle of Avès, beside the Spanish main.

There were forty craft in Avès that were both swift and stout,
All furnished well with small arms and cannons round about;
And a thousand men in Avès made laws so fair and free
To choose their valiant captains and obey them loyally.

Thence we sailed against the Spaniard with his hoards of plate
    and gold,
Which he wrung by cruel tortures from the Indian folk of old;
Likewise the merchant captains, with hearts as hard as stone,
Which flog men and keel-haul them and starve them to the bone.

Oh the palms grew high in Avès, and fruits that shone like gold,
And the colibris and parrots they were gorgeous to behold;
And the negro maids to Avès from bondage fast did flee,
To welcome gallant sailors, a-sweeping in from sea.

Oh sweet it was in Avès to hear the landward breeze
A-swing with good tobacco in a net between the trees,
With a negro lass to fan you, while you listened to the roar
Of the breakers on the reef outside that never touched the shore.

But Scripture saith, an ending to all fine things must be;
So the King's ships sailed on Avès, and quite put down were we.
All day we fought like bulldogs, but they burst the booms at night;
And I fled in a piragua, sore wounded, from the fight.

Nine days I floated starving, and a negro lass beside,
Till for all I tried to cheer her, the poor young thing she died;
But as I lay a gasping, a Bristol sail came by,
And brought me home to England here, to beg until I die.

And now I'm old and going – I'm sure I can't tell where;
One comfort is, this world's so hard, I can't be worse off there:
If I might but be a sea-dove, I'd fly across the main,
To the pleasant Isle of Avès, to look at it once again.

Charles Kingsley (1819–75)

The Private of the Buffs

Last night, among his fellow roughs,
　　He jested, quaffed, and swore;
A drunken private of the Buffs,
　　Who never looked before.
Today, beneath the foeman's frown,
　　He stands in Elgin's place,
Ambassador from Britain's crown
　　And type of all her race.

Poor, reckless, rude, low-born, untaught,
　　Bewildered, and alone,
A heart with English instinct fraught
　　He yet can call his own.
Aye, tear his body limb from limb,
　　Bring cord, or axe, or flame:
He only knows, that not through him
　　Shall England come to shame.

Far Kentish hop-fields round him seemed,
　　Like dreams, to come and go;
Bright leagues of cherry-blossom gleamed,
　　One sheet of living snow;
The smoke above his father's door
　　In grey soft eddyings hung:
Must he then watch it rise no more,
　　Doomed by himself, so young?

Yes, honour calls! – with strength like steel
  He puts the vision by.
Let dusky Indians whine and kneel;
  An English lad must die.
And thus, with eyes that would not shrink,
  With knee to man unbent,
Unfaltering on its dreadful brink,
  To his red grave he went.

Vain, mightiest fleets of iron framed;
  Vain, those all-shattering guns;
Unless proud England keep, untamed,
  The strong heart of her sons.
So, let his name through Europe ring –
  A man of mean estate,
Who died, as firm as Sparta's king,
  Because his soul was great.

Sir Francis Hastings Doyle (1810–88)

Men Who March Away
(Song of the Soldiers)

What of the faith and fire within us
 Men who march away
 Ere the barn-cocks say
 Night is growing gray,
Leaving all that here can win us;
What of the faith and fire within us
 Men who march away?

Is it a purblind prank, O think you,
 Friend with the musing eye,
 Who watch us stepping by
 With doubt and dolorous sigh?
Can much pondering so hoodwink you!
Is it a purblind prank, O think you,
 Friend with the musing eye?

Nay. We see well what we are doing,
 Though some may not see –
 Dalliers as they be –
 England's need are we;
Her distress would leave us rueing:
Nay. We well see what we are doing,
 Though some may not see!

In our heart of hearts believing
 Victory crowns the just,
 And that braggarts must

Surely bite the dust,
Press we to the field ungrieving,
In our heart of hearts believing
   Victory crowns the just.

Hence the faith and fire within us
   Men who march away
   Ere the barn-cocks say
   Night is growing gray,
Leaving all that here can win us;
Hence the faith and fire within us
   Men who march away.

Thomas Hardy (1840–1928)

'Trail all your pikes'

Trail all your pikes, dispirit every drum,
March in a slow procession from afar,
Ye silent, ye dejected men of war!
Be still the hautboys, and the flute be dumb!
Display no more, in vain, the loftly banner.
For see! where on the bier before ye lies
The pale, the fallen the untimely sacrifice
To your mistaken shrine, to your false idol Honour!

All Is Vanity
Anne Finch, Countess of Winchilsea (1661–1720)

The Charge of the Light Brigade

Half a league, half a league,
Half a league onward,
All in the valley of death
  Rode the six hundred.
  'Forward, the Light Brigade!
Charge for the guns!' he said.
Into the valley of death
  Rode the six hundred.

'Forward, the Light Brigade!'
Was there a man dismayed?
Not though the soldier knew
  Some one had blundered.
Theirs not to make reply,
Theirs not to reason why,
Theirs but to do and die.
Into the valley of death
  Rode the six hundred.

Cannon to right of them,
Cannon to left of them,
Cannon in front of them
  Volleyed and thundered;
Stormed at with shot and shell,
Boldly they rode and well,
Into the jaws of death,
Into the mouth of hell
  Rode the six hundred.

Flashed all their sabres bare,
Flashed as they turned in air,
Sabring the gunners there,
    Charging an army, while
All the world wondered:
Plunged in the battery-smoke
Right through the line they broke;
Cossack and Russian
Reeled from the sabre-stroke
Shattered and sundered.
Then they rode back, but not,
    Not the six hundred.

Cannon to right of them,
Cannon to left of them,
Cannon behind them
    Volleyed and thundered;
Stormed at with shot and shell,
While horse and hero fell,
They that had fought so well
Came through the jaws of death
Back from the mouth of hell,
All that was left of them,
    Left of six hundred.

When can their glory fade?
O the wild charge they made!
    All the world wondered.
Honour the charge they made!
Honour the Light Brigade,
    Noble six hundred!

Alfred, Lord Tennyson (1809–92)

Dulce et Decorum Est

Bent double, like old beggars under sacks,
Knock-kneed, coughing like hags, we cursed through sludge,
Till on the haunting flares we turned our backs
And towards our distant rest began to trudge.
Men marched asleep. Many had lost their boots
But limped on, blood-shod. All went lame; all blind;
Drunk with fatigue; deaf even to the hoots
Of tired, outstripped Five-Nines that dropped behind.

Gas! GAS! Quick, boys! – An ecstasy of fumbling,
Fitting the clumsy helmets just in time;
But someone still was yelling out and stumbling,
And floundering like a man in fire or lime ...
Dim, through the misty panes and thick green light,
As under a green sea, I saw him drowning.

In all my dreams, before my helpless sight,
He plunges at me, guttering, choking, drowning.

If in some smothering dreams you too could pace
Behind the wagon that we flung him in,
And watch the white eyes writhing in his face,
His hanging face, like a devil's sick of sin;
If you could hear, at every jolt, the blood
Come gargling from the froth-corrupted lungs,
Obscene as cancer, bitter as the cud
Of vile, incurable sores on innocent tongues, –
My friend, you would not tell with such high zest
To children ardent for some desperate glory,
The old Lie; Dulce et Decorum est
Pro patria mori.

Wilfred Owen (1893–1918)

Remembrance

David's Lament over Saul and Jonathan

The beauty of Israel is slain upon thy high places: how are the mighty fallen!

Tell it not in Gath, publish it not in the streets of Askelon: lest the daughters of the Philistines rejoice, lest the daughters of the uncircumcised triumph.

Ye mountains of Gilboa, let there be no dew, neither let there be rain, upon you, nor fields of offerings: for there the shield of the mighty is vilely cast away, he shield of Saul, as though he had not been anointed with oil.

From the blood of the slain, from the fat of the mighty, the bow of Jonathan turned not back, and the sword of Saul returned not empty.

Saul and Jonathan were lovely and pleasant in their lives, and in their death they were not divided: they were swifter than eagles, they were stronger than lions.

Ye daughters of Israel, weep over Saul, who clothed you in scarlet, with other delights; who put on ornaments of gold upon your apparel.

How are the mighty fallen in the midst of the battle! O Jonathan, thou wast slain in thine high places.

I am distressed for thee, my brother Jonathan: very pleasant hast thou been unto me: thy love to me was wonderful, passing the love of women.

How are the mighty fallen, and the weapons of war perished!

The Bible, Samuel 2
The King James Version (1611)

The Burial of Sir John Moore
after Corunna

Not a drum was heard, not a funeral note,
    As his corpse to the rampart we hurried;
Not a soldier discharged his farewell shot
    Over the grave where our hero we buried.

We buried him darkly at dead of night,
    The sods with our bayonets turning,
By the struggling moonbeam's misty light
    And the lanthorn dimly burning.

No useless coffin enclosed his breast,
    Not in sheet or in shroud we wound him;
But he lay like a warrior taking his rest
    With his martial cloak around him.

Few and short were the prayers we said,
    And we spoke not a word of sorrow;
But we steadfastly gazed on the face that was dead,
    And we bitterly thought of the morrow.

We thought, as we hollowed his narrow bed
    And smoothed down his lonely pillow,
That the foe and the stranger would tread o'er his head,
    And we far away on the billow!

Lightly they'll talk of the spirit that's gone,
   And o'er his cold ashes upbraid him –
But little he'll reck, if they let him sleep on
   In the grave where a Briton has laid him.

But half of our heavy task was done
   When the clock struck the hour for retiring;
And we heard the distant and random gun
   That the foe was sullenly firing.

Slowly and sadly we laid him down,
   From the field of his fame fresh and gory;
We carved not a line, and we raised not a stone,
   But we left him alone with his glory.

                              Charles Wolfe (1791–1823)

Drummer Hodge

I

They throw in Drummer Hodge, to rest
  Uncoffined – just as found:
His landmark is a kopje-crest
  That breaks the veldt around;
And foreign constellations west
  Each night above his mound.

II

Young Hodge the Drummer never knew –
  Fresh from his Wessex home –
The meaning of the broad Karoo,
  The Bush, the dusty loam,
And why uprose to nightly view
  Strange stars amid the gloam.

III

Yet portion of that unknown plain
  Will Hodge for ever be;
His homely Northern breast and brain
  Grow to some Southern tree,
And strange-eyed constellation reign
  His stars eternally.

Thomas Hardy (1840–1928)

A Private

This ploughman dead in battle slept out of doors
Many a frozen night, and merrily
Answered staid drinkers, good bedmen, and all bores:
'At Mrs Greenland's Hawthorn Bush,' said he,
'I slept.' None knew which bush. Above the town,
Beyond 'The Drover', a hundred spot the down
In Wiltshire. And where now at last he sleeps
More sound in France – that, too, he secret keeps.

Edward Thomas (1878–1917)

The Cenotaph
September 1919

Not yet will those measureless fields be green again
Where only yesterday the wild sweet blood of wonderful
    youth was shed;
There is a grave whose earth must hold too long, too deep
    a stain,
Though for ever over it we may speak as proudly as we
    may tread.
But here, where the watchers by lonely hearths from the
    thrust of an inward sword have more slowly bled,
We shall build the cenotaph: victory, winged, with peace,
    winged too, at the column's head.
And over the stairway, at the foot – oh! here, leave
    desolate, passionate hands to spread
Violets, roses, and laurel, with the small, sweet, twinkling
    country things
Speaking so wistfully of other springs,
From the little gardens of little places where son or
    sweetheart was born and bred.
In splendid sleep, with a thousand brothers
       To lovers – to mothers
       Here, too, lies he:
Under the purple, the green, the red,
It is all young life: it must break some women's hearts to see
Such a brave, gay coverlet to such a bed!
Only, when all is done and said,
God is not mocked and neither are the dead

For this will stand in our market-place –
      Who'll sell, who'll buy?
      (Will you or I
Lie each to each with the better grace?)
While looking into every busy whore's and huckster's face
As they drive their bargains, is the face
Of God: and some young, piteous, murdered face.

Charlotte Mew (1869–1928)

Concord Hymn

By the rude bridge that arched the flood,
  Their flag to April's breeze unfurled,
Here once the embattled farmers stood,
  And fired the shot heard round the world.

The foe long since in silence slept;
  Alike the conqueror silent sleeps;
And Time the ruined bridge has swept
  Down the dark stream which seaward creeps.

On this green bank, by this soft stream,
  We set today a votive stone;
That memory may their deed redeem,
  When, like our sires, our sons are gone.

Spirit, that made those heroes dare
  To die, and leave their children free,
Bid Time and Nature gently spare
  The shaft we raise to them and thee.

Ralph Waldo Emerson (1803–82)

Gettysburg

Fourscore and seven years ago our fathers brought forth upon this continent a new nation, conceived in liberty, and dedicated to the proposition that all men are created equal. Now we are engaged in a great civil war, testing whether that nation, or any nation so conceived and so dedicated, can long endure. We are met on a great battlefield of that war. We have come to dedicate a portion of that field as a final resting place of those who here gave their lives that that nation might live. It is altogether fitting and proper that we should do this. But in a larger sense we cannot dedicate, we cannot consecrate, we cannot hallow this ground. The brave men, living and dead, who struggled here, have consecrated it far above our power to add or detract. The world will little note, nor long remember, what we say here, but it can never forget what they did here. It is for us, the living, rather to be dedicated here to the unfinished work they have thus far so nobly advanced. It is rather for us to be here dedicated to the great task remaining before us, that from these honoured dead we take increased devotion to that cause for which they gave the last full measure of devotion; that we here highly resolve that the dead shall not have died in vain, that the nation shall, under God, have a new birth of freedom, and that government of the people, by the people, and for the people, shall not perish from the earth.

Dedicatory Address at Gettysburg Cemetery
Abraham Lincoln (1809–65)

When You See Millions of the Mouthless Dead

When you see millions of the mouthless dead
Across your dreams in pale battalions go,
Say not soft things as other men have said,
That you'll remember. For you need not so.
Give them not praise. For, deaf, how should they know
It is not curses heaped on each gashed head?
Nor tears. Their blind eyes see not your tears flow.
Nor honour. It is easy to be dead.
Say only this, 'They are dead.' Then add thereto,
'Yet many a better one has died before.'
Then scanning all the overcrowded mass, should you
Perceive one face that you loved heretofore,
It is a spook. None wears the face you knew.
Great death has made all his for evermore.

Charles Hamilton Sorley (1895–1915)

Anthem for Doomed Youth

What passing-bells for these who die as cattle?
  Only the monstrous anger of the guns.
Only the stuttering rifles' rapid rattle
  Can patter out their hasty orisons.
No mockeries for them; no prayers nor bells,
  Nor any voice of mourning save the choirs, –
The shrill, demented choirs of wailing shells;
  And bugles calling for them from sad shires.

What candles may be held to speed them all?
  Not in the hands of boys, but in their eyes
  Shall shine the holy glimmers of good-byes.
The pallor of girls' brows shall be their pall;
  Their flowers the tenderness of silent minds,
  And each slow dusk a drawing-down of blinds.

Wilfred Owen (1893–1918)

In Flanders Fields

In Flanders fields the poppies blow
Between the crosses, row on row,
That mark our place; and in the sky
The larks, still bravely singing, fly
Scarce heard amid the guns below.

We are the dead. Short days ago
We lived, felt dawn, saw sunset glow,
Loved and were loved, and now we lie
In Flanders fields.

Take up our quarrel with the foe:
To you from failing hands we throw
The torch; be yours to hold it high.
If ye break faith with us who die
We shall not sleep, though poppies grow
In Flanders fields.

John McCrae (1872–1918)

In Memoriam
Easter 1915

The flowers left thick at nightfall in the wood
This Eastertide call into mind the men,
Now far from home, who, with their sweethearts, should
Have gathered them and will do never again.

Edward Thomas (1878–1917)

Futility

Move him into the sun –
Gently its touch awoke him once,
At home, whispering of fields unsown.
Always it woke him, even in France,
Until this morning and this snow.
If anything might rouse him now
The kind old sun will know.

Think how it wakes the seeds, –
Woke, once, the clays of a cold star.
Are limbs, so dear-achieved, are sides,
Full-nerved, – still warm, – too hard to stir?
Was it for this the clay grew tall?
– O what made fatuous sunbeams toil
To break earth's sleep at all?

Wilfred Owen (1893–1918)

The Sun Used to Shine

The sun used to shine while we two walked
Slowly together, paused and started
Again, and sometimes mused, sometimes talked
As either pleased, and cheerfully parted

Each night. We never disagreed
Which gate to rest on. The to be
And the late past we gave small heed.
We turned from men or poetry

To rumours of the war remote
Only till both stood disinclined
For aught but the yellow flavorous coat
Of an apple wasps had undermined;

Or a sentry of dark betonies,
The stateliest of small flowers on earth,
At the forest verge; or crocuses
Pale purple as if they had their birth

In sunless Hades fields. The war
Came back to mind with the moonrise
Which soldiers in the east afar
Beheld then. Nevertheless, our eyes

Could as well imagine the Crusades
Or Caesar's battles. Everything
To faintness like those rumours fades –
Like the brook's water glittering

Under the moonlight – like those walks
Now – like us two that took them, and
The fallen apples, all the talks
And silences – like memory's sand

When the tide covers it late or soon,
And other men through other flowers
In those fields under the same moon
Go talking and have easy hours.

Edward Thomas (1878–1917)

In Times of Wars and Tumults

'Would that I'd not drawn breath here!' someone said,
'To stalk upon this stage of evil deeds,
Where purposelessly month by month proceeds
A play so sorely shaped and blood-bespread.'

Yet had his spark not quickened, but lain dead
To the gross spectacles of this our day,
And never put on the proffered cloak of clay,
He had but not known things now manifested;

Life would have swirled the same. Morns would have
dawned
On the uprooting by the night-gun's stroke
Of what the yester noonshine brought to flower;

Brown martial brows in dying throes have wanned
Despite his absence; hearts no fewer been broke
By Empery's insatiate lust of power.

Thomas Hardy (1840–1928)

It Feels a Shame to Be Alive

It feels a shame to be Alive –
When Men so brave – are dead –
One envies the Distinguished Dust –
Permitted – such a Head –

The Stone – that tells defending Whom
This Spartan put away
What little of Him we – possessed
In Pawn for Liberty –

The price is great – Sublimely paid –
Do we deserve – a Thing –
That lives – like Dollars – must be piled
Before we may obtain?

Are we that wait – sufficient worth –
That such Enormous Pearl
As life – dissolved be – for Us –
In Battle's – horrid Bowl?

It may be – a Renown to live –
I think the Men who die –
Those unsustained – Saviours –
Present Divinity –

Emily Dickinson (1830–86)

Evening Thoughts after Wartime

Walking one day toward the village, as we used to call it in the good old days when almost every dweller in the town had been born in it, I was enjoying that delicious sense of disenthralment from the actual which the deepening twilight brings with it, giving as it does a sort of obscure novelty to things familiar. The coolness, the hush, broken only by the distant bleat of some belated goat, querulous to be disburdened of her milky load, the few faint stars, more guessed as yet than seen, the sense that the coming dark would so soon fold me in the secure privacy of its disguise, – all things combined in a result as near absolute peace as can be hoped for by a man who knows that there is a writ out against him in the hands of the printer's devil. For the moment, I was enjoying the blessed privilege of thinking, without being called on to stand and deliver what I thought to the small public, who are good enough to take any interest therein.

I love old ways, and the path I was walking felt kindly to the feet it had known for almost fifty years. How many fleeting impressions it had shared with me! How many times I had lingered to study the shadows of the leaves mezzotinted upon the turf that edged it by the moon, of the bare boughs etched with a touch beyond Rembrandt by the same unconscious artist on the smooth page of snow! If I turned round, through dusky tree-gaps came the first twinkle of evening lamps in the dear old homestead. On Corey's hill I could see these tiny pharoses of love and home and sweet domestic thoughts flash out one by one across the blackening salt-meadow between. How much has not kerosene added to the cheerfulness of our evening landscape! A pair of night

137

herons flapped heavily over me toward the hidden river. The war was ended. I might walk townward without that aching dread of bulletins that had darkened the July sunshine and twice made the scarlet leaves of October seem stained with blood. I remembered with a pang, half-proud, half-painful, how, so many years ago, I had walked over the same path and felt round my finger the soft pressure of a little hand that was one day to harden with faithful grip of sabre. On how many paths, leading to how many homes where proud Memory does all she can to fill up the fireside gaps with shining shapes, must not men be walking in just such pensive mood as I? Ah, young heroes, safe in immortal youth as those of Homer, you at least carried your ideal hence untarnished! It is locked for you beyond moth or rust in the treasure-chamber of Death.

On a Certain Condescension in Foreigners
James Russell Lowell (1819–91)

February Afternoon

Men heard this roar of parleying starlings, saw,
  A thousand years ago even as now,
  Black rooks with white gulls following the plough
So that the first are last until a caw
Commands that last are first again, – a law
  Which was of old when one, like me, dreamed how
  A thousand years might dust lie on his brow
Yet thus would birds do between hedge and shaw.

Time swims before me, making as a day
  A thousand years, while the broad ploughland oak
  Roars mill-like and men strike and bear the stroke
  Of war as ever, audacious or resigned,
And God still sits aloft in the array
  That we have wrought him, stone-deaf and stone-blind.

Edward Thomas (1878–1917)

Peace

In Time of 'The Breaking of Nations'

I

Only a man harrowing clods
  In a slow silent walk
With an old horse that stumbles and nods
  Half asleep as they stalk.

II

Only thin smoke without flame
  From the heaps of couch-grass;
Yet this will go onwards the same
  Though dynasties pass.

III

Yonder a maid and her wight
  Come whispering by:
War's annals will cloud into night
  Ere their story die.

Thomas Hardy (1840–1928)

Peace

My soul, there is a country
  Far beyond the stars,
Where stands a wingèd sentry
  All skilful in the wars:
There, above noise and danger,
  Sweet Peace sits crowned with smiles,
And one born in a manger
  Commands the beauteous files.
He is thy gracious friend,
  And – O my soul, awake! –
Did in pure love descend
  To die here for thy sake.
If thou canst get but thither,
  There grows the flower of Peace,
The rose that cannot wither,
  Thy fortress, and thy ease.
Leave then thy foolish ranges;
  For none can thee secure
But one who never changes –
  Thy God, thy life, thy cure.

Henry Vaughan (1621–95)

Peace

Sweet Peace, where dost thou dwell? I humbly crave,
　　　　Let me once know.
　　I sought thee in a secret cave,
　　　　And asked, if Peace were there.
A hollow wind did seem to answer, No:
　　　　Go seek elsewhere.

I did; and going did a rainbow note:
　　　　Surely, thought I,
　　This is the lace of Peace's coat:
　　　　I will search out the matter.
But while I looked, the clouds immediately
　　　　Did break and scatter.

Then went I to a garden, and did spy
　　　　A gallant flower,
　　The crown imperial: Sure, said I,
　　　　Peace at the root must dwell.
But when I digged, I saw a worm devour
　　　　What showed so well.

At length I met a reverend good old man,
　　　　Whom when for Peace
　　I did demand; he thus began:
　　　　There was a prince of old
At Salem dwelt, who lived with good increase
　　　　Of flock and fold.

He sweetly lived; yet sweetness did not save
        His life from foes.
  But after death out of his grave
        There sprang twelve stalks of wheat:
Which many wondering at, got some of those
        To plant and set.

It prospered strangely, and did soon disperse
        Through all the earth:
  For they that taste it do rehearse,
        That virtue lies therein,
A secret virtue bringing Peace and mirth
        By flight of sin.

Take of this grain, which in my garden grows,
        And grows for you;
  Make bread of it: and that repose
        And Peace which every where
With so much earnestness you do pursue,
        Is only there.

               George Herbert (1593–1633)

Autumn Sunset

The sun sets on some retired meadow, where no house is visible, with all the glory and splendour that it lavishes on cities, and, perchance, as it has never set before, – where there is but a solitary marsh hawk to have his wings gilded by it, or only a musquash looks out from his cabin, and there is some little black-veined brook in the midst of the marsh, just beginning to meander, winding slowly round a decaying stump. We walked in so pure and bright a light, gilding the withered grass and leaves, so softly and serenely bright, I thought I had never bathed in such a golden flood, without a ripple or a murmur to it. The west side of every wood and rising ground gleamed like the boundary of Elysium, and the sun on our backs seemed like a gentle herdsman driving us home at evening.

So we saunter toward the Holy Land, till one day the sun shall shine more brightly than ever he has done, shall perchance shine into our minds and hearts, and light up our whole lives with a great awakening light, as warm and serene and golden as on a bank side in autumn.

Walking
Henry Thoreau (1817–62)

The Garden

How vainly men themselves amaze
To win the palm, the oak, or bays;
And their incessant labours see
Crowned from some single herb or tree.
Whose short and narrow verged shade
Does prudently their toils upbraid;
While all flowers and all trees do close
To weave the garlands of repose.

Fair quiet, have I found thee here,
And innocence thy sister dear!
Mistaken long, I sought you then
In busy companies of men.
Your sacred plants, if here below,
Only among the plants will grow.
Society is all but rude,
To this delicious solitude.

No white nor red was ever seen
So amorous as this lovely green.
Fond lovers, cruel as their flame,
Cut in these trees their mistress' name.
Little, alas, they know, or heed,
How far these beauties hers exceed!
Fair trees! where so ever your barks I wound,
No name shall but your own be found.

When we have run our passion's heat,
Love hither makes his best retreat.

The gods, that mortal beauty chase,
Still in a tree did end their race.
Apollo hunted Daphne so,
Only that she might laurel grow.
And Pan did after Syrinx speed,
Not as a nymph, but for a reed.

What wonderous life in this I lead!
Ripe apples drop about my head;
The luscious clusters of the vine
Upon my mouth do crush their wine;
The nectarine, and curious peach,
Into my hands themselves do reach;
Stumbling on melons, as I pass,
Insnared with flowers, I fall on grass.

Meanwhile the mind, from pleasure less,
Withdraws into its happiness:
The mind, that ocean where each kind
Does straight its own resemblance find;
Yet it creates, transcending these,
Far other worlds, and other seas;
Annihilating all that's made
To a green thought in a green shade.

Here at the fountain's sliding foot,
Or at some fruit trees mossy root,
Casting the body's vest aside,
My soul into the boughs does glide:
There like a bird it sits, and sings,
Then whets, and combs its silver wings;

And, till prepared for longer flight,
Waves in its plumes the various light.

Such was that happy garden-state,
While man there walked without a mate:
After a place so pure, and sweet,
What other help could yet be meet!
But 'twas beyond a mortal's share
To wander solitary there:
Two paradises 'twere in one
To live in paradise alone.

How well the skilful gardener drew
Of flowers and herbs this dial new;
Where from above the milder sun
Does through a fragrant zodiac run;
And, as it works, the industrious bee
Computes its time as well as we.
How could such sweet and wholesome hours
Be reckoned but with herbs and flowers!

Andrew Marvell (1621–78)

My Mind to Me a Kingdom Is

My mind to me a kingdom is,
  Such present joys therein I find,
That it excels all other bliss
  That earth affords or grows by kind.
Though much I want which most would have,
Yet still my mind forbids to crave.

No princely pomp, no wealthy store,
  No force to win the victory,
No wily wit to salve a sore,
  No shape to feed a loving eye;
To none of these I yield as thrall,
For why my mind doth serve for all.

I see how plenty suffers oft,
  And hasty climbers soon do fall;
I see that which are aloft
  Mishap doth threaten most of all;
These get with toil, they keep with fear:
Such cares my mind can never bear.

Content I live, this is my stay,
  I see no more than may suffice;
I press to bear no haughty sway;
  Look, what I lack my mind supplies.
Lo! this I triumph like a king,
Content with that my mind doth bring.

Some have too much, but still do crave;
   I have little, and seek no more.
They are but poor, though much they have.
   And I am rich with little store.
They poor, I rich; they beg, I give;
They lack, I leave; they pine, I live.

I laugh not at another's loss;
   I grudge not at another's gain;
No worldly waves my mind can toss;
   My state at one doth still remain.
I fear no foe, I fawn on friend,
I loathe not life, nor dread my end.

Some weigh their pleasure by their lust.
   Their wisdom by their rage of will;
Their treasure is their only trust,
   A cloakèd craft their store of skill:
But all the pleasure that I find
Is to maintain a quiet mind.

My wealth is health and perfect ease,
   My conscience clear my choice defence;
I neither seek by bribes to please,
   Nor by deceit to breed offence.
Thus do I live; thus will I die;
Would all did so as well as I!

Sir Edward Dyer (1543–1607)

Abou Ben Adhem and the Angel

Abou Ben Adhem (may his tribe increase!)
Awoke one night from a deep dream of peace,
And saw, within the moonlight in his room,
Making it rich, and like a lily in bloom,
An angel writing in a book of gold: –
Exceeding peace had made Ben Adhem bold,
And to presence in the room he said,
  'What writest thou?' – The vision raised its head,
And with a look made of all sweet accord,
Answered, 'The names of those who love the Lord.'
'And is mine one?' said Abou. 'Nay, not so,'
Replied the angel. Abou spoke more low,
But cheerly still; and said, 'I pray thee, then,
Write me as one that loves his fellow men.'
  The angel wrote, and vanished. The next night
It came again with a great wakening light,
And showed the names whom love of God had blest,
And lo! Ben Adhem's name led all the rest!

Leigh Hunt (1784–1859)

A Child's Vision of the World

Will you see the infancy of this sublime and celestial greatness? Those pure and virgin apprehensions I had from the womb, and that divine light wherewith I was born are the best unto this day, wherein I can see the universe. By the gift of God they attended me into the world, and by His special favour I remember them till now. Verily they seem the greatest gifts His wisdom could bestow, for without them all other gifts had been dead and vain. They are unattainable by book, and therefore I will teach them by experience. Pray for them earnestly: for they will make you angelical, and wholly celestial. Certainly Adam in paradise had not more sweet and curious apprehensions of the world, than I when I was a child.

All appeared new, and strange at first, inexpressibly rare and delightful and beautiful. I was a little stranger, which at my entrance into the world was saluted and surrounded with innumerable joys. My knowledge was divine. I knew by intuition those things which since my apostasy, I collected again by the highest reason. My very ignorance was advantageous. I seemed as one brought into the estate of innocence. All things were spotless and pure and glorious: yea, and infinitely mine, and joyful and precious. I knew not that there were any sins, or complaints or laws. I dreamed not of poverties, contentions or vices. All tears and quarrels were hidden from mine eyes. Everything was at rest, free and immortal. I knew nothing of sickness or death or rents or exaction, either for tribute or bread. In the absence of these I was entertained like an angel with the works of God in their splendour and glory, I saw all in the peace of Eden; Heaven and Earth did sing my Creator's praises, and could not make more melody to Adam, than to me. All time was eternity, and a perpetual sabbath. Is it not strange, that an infant should be heir of the whole world, and see those mysteries which the books of the learned never unfold?

The corn was orient and immortal wheat, which never should be reaped, nor was ever sown. I thought it had stood from everlasting to everlasting. The dust and stones of the street were as precious as gold: the gates were at first the end of the world. The green trees when I saw them first through one of the gates transported and ravished me, their sweetness and unusual beauty made my heart to leap, and almost mad with ecstasy, they were such strange and wonderful things. The men! O what venerable and reverend creatures did the aged seem! Immortal cherubims! And young men glittering and sparkling angels, and maids strange seraphic pieces of life and beauty! Boys and girls tumbling in the street, and playing, were moving jewels. I knew not that they were born or should die; but all things abided eternally as they were in their proper places. Eternity was manifest in the light of the day, and something infinite behind everything appeared which talked with my expectation and moved my desire. The city seemed to stand in Eden, or to be built in heaven. The streets were mine, the temple was mine, the people were mine, their clothes and gold and silver were mine, as much as their sparkling eyes, fair skins and ruddy faces. The skies were mine, and so were the sun and moon and stars, and all the world was mine; and I the only spectator and enjoyer of it.

Centuries of Meditations
Thomas Traherne (1637–74)

The Earthly Paradise

Of heaven or hell I have no power to sing,
I cannot ease the burden of your fears,
Or make quick-coming death a little thing,
Or bring again the pleasure of past years,
Nor for my words shall ye forget your tears,
Or hope again for aught that I can say,
The idle singer of an empty day.

But rather, when aweary of your mirth,
From full hearts still unsatisfied ye sigh,
And, feeling kindly unto all the earth,
Grudge every minute as it passes by,
Made the more mindful that the sweet days die –
Remember me a little then, I pray,
The idle singer of an empty day.

The heavy trouble, the bewildering care
That weighs us down who live and earn our bread,
These idle verses have no power to bear;
So let me sing of names remembered,
Because they, living not, can never be dead,
Or long time take their memory quite away
From us poor singers of an empty day.

Dreamer of dreams, born out of my due time,
Why should I strive to set the crooked straight?
Let it suffice me that my murmuring rhyme
Beats with light wing against the ivory gate,
Telling a tale not too importunate

To those who in the sleepy region stay,
Lulled by the singer of an empty day.

Folk say, a wizard to a northern king
At Christmas-tide such wondrous things did show,
That through one window men beheld the spring,
And through another saw the summer glow,
And through a third the fruited vines a-row,
While still, unheard, but in its wonted way,
Piped the drear wind of that December day.

So with this earthly paradise it is,
If ye will read aright, and pardon me,
Who strive to build a shadowy isle of bliss
Midmost the beating of the steely sea,
Where tossed about all hearts of men must be;
Whose ravening monsters mighty men shall slay,
Not the poor singer of an empty day.

William Morris (1834–96)

The Garden of Eden

So hand in hand they passed, the loveliest pair
That ever since in love's embraces met,
Adam the goodliest man of men since born
His sons, the fairest of her daughters Eve.
Under a tuft of shade that on a green
Stood whispering soft, by a fresh fountain side
They sat them down, and after no more toil
Of their sweet gardening labour than sufficed
To recommend cool zephyr, and made ease
More easy, wholesome thirst and appetite
More grateful, to their supper fruits they fell,
Nectarine fruits which the compliant boughs
Yielded them, sidelong as they sat recline
On the soft downy bank damasked with flowers:
The savoury pulp they chew, and in the rind
Still as they thirsted scoop the brimming stream;
Nor gentle purpose, nor endearing smiles
Wanted, nor youthful dalliance as beseems
Fair couple, linked in happy nuptial league,
Alone as they.

Paradise Lost, Book IV
John Milton (1608–74)

Peace

When will you ever, Peace, wild wood dove, shy wings shut,
Your round me roaming end, and under be my boughs?
When, when, Peace, will you, Peace? I'll not play hypocrite
To own my heart: I yield you do come sometimes; but
That piecemeal peace is poor peace. What pure peace allows
Alarms of wars, the daunting wars, the death of it?

O surely, reaving Peace, my Lord should leave in lieu
Some good! And so he does leave patience exquisite,
That plumes to peace thereafter. And when Peace here does house
He comes with work to do, he does not come to coo,
    He comes to brood and sit.

Gerard Manley Hopkins (1844–89)

Christmas: 1924

'Peace upon earth!' was said. We sing it,
And pay a million priests to bring it.
After two thousand years of mass
We've got as far as poison-gas.

Thomas Hardy (1840–1928)

Ring Out, Wild Bells

Ring out, wild bells, to the wild sky,
The flying cloud, the frosty light:
The year is dying in the night;
Ring out, wild bells, and let him die.

Ring out the old, ring in the new,
Ring, happy bells, across the snow:
The year is going, let him go;
Ring out the false, ring in the true.

Ring out the grief that saps the mind,
For those that here we see no more;
Ring out the feud of rich and poor,
Ring in redress to all mankind.

Ring out a slowly dying cause,
And ancient forms of party strife;
Ring in the nobler modes of life,
With sweeter manners, purer laws.

Ring out the want, the care, the sin,
The faithless coldness of the times;
Ring out, ring out my mournful rhymes,
But ring the fuller minstrel in.

Ring out false pride in place and blood,
The civic slander and the spite;
Ring in the love of truth and right,
Ring in the common love of good.

Ring out old shapes of foul disease;
Ring out the narrowing lust of gold;
Ring out the thousand wars of old,
Ring in the thousand years of peace.

Ring in the valiant man and free,
The larger heart, the kindlier hand;
Ring out the darkness of the land,
Ring in the Christ that is to be.

In Memoriam
Alfred, Lord Tennyson (1809–92)

Index of First Lines

Index of Authors